Directions To Heaven

Revised Second Edition

Michael Regan

Directions to Heaven
Copyright © 2019, Revised 2021, Second Edition 2022
Revised Second Edition 2025
by: Michael Regan

ISBN: 979-8-218-58077-3

Dedication

With all my love and admiration
to my mother and father, and to
the memory of Dr. D. James Kennedy,
my favorite pastor.

Contents

To Buy, go to:

directionstoheaven.org

Forward

Truth: **God is truth, and life**. "I am the way and the truth and the life. No one comes to the Father except through me" (John 14:6).

Lies: **Satan is lies, and death**. "He was a murderer from the beginning, not holding to the truth, for there is no truth in him. When he lies, he speaks his native language, for he is a liar and the father of lies" (John 8:44).

The Bible is true. It contains words of the *only* God.

"Before me no god was formed, nor will there be one after me" (Isaiah 43:10).

"I am the first and I am the last; apart from me there is no God" (Isaiah 44:6).

The Bible is true. It is true because it has been proven to be true. It has been proven by history. It has been proven by archaeology. It has been proven time, and time again by the hundreds of clear and absolute examples of fulfilled prophecies.

The only road to heaven, is the way of Jesus Christ. "Salvation is found in no one else, for there is no other name under heaven given to mankind by which we must be saved" (Acts 4:12).

Be a Berean! This is of high importance for all Christians. Be a Berean. The Bereans are mentioned in the 17th chapter of Acts. "Now the Berean Jews were of more noble character than those in Thessalonica, for they received the message with great eagerness and examined the Scriptures every day to see if what Paul said was true. As a result, many of them believed, as did also a number of prominent Greek women and many Greek men" (Acts 17:11,12).

How can we know what to believe, and what not to believe? Know the Bible. Don't just read it. Know it. Be a Berean and examine the scriptures daily. When you read it, two things are important. Read it slowly and carefully. Seriously consider what it is that you are reading, and understand it to the best of your ability. The first and most important is to read and understand the Bible. Secondly, after reading and understanding, you should put it into your active memory. Remember it. How else can you depend on the promises of God, if you can't remember what he said? How can you share your faith with others if you do not remember the words of God? None of us have perfect memories, but we all can remember a few things that are important to us. For information that is vitally important, you went over and over those things until they were committed to your memory. We can remember things that are important. God's word in the Bible has vital importance. You will find certain scriptures that are especially important to you. Your interest in them makes memory easier. Just go over and over them several times, underline or highlight them. They will stand out in your memory. As you continue to read and have a better understanding of who he is, and his guidance for you. The more you know of God, and the richness he offers in Jesus Christ, the more fulfilled you will be, and the more eager to share this wealth with others. In the absence of perfect memory, most of us "paraphrase". We tell it to the best of our memory. Know the Bible. Know what you believe, and what you don't believe, and why. Be a Berean.

Chapter 1

Beginnings

Why?

Today, the United States of America, that from its inception, was emphatically a Christian nation, is now in the process of going the way of Cain. Why?

What I find to be enormously disappointing is that today's Christian churches in America are not telling us so. They all seem to be terrified of being offensive. They hide behind the skirts of Political Correctness. Very few will ever preach against sin, even though sin is killing us. It is tearing down our families, churches, institutions of learning, corporations, and politics. How far have we fallen? An excellent book which documents the Christian foundation of each of the colonies, and the young country under the newly written Constitution, is: *For God And Country*[1] by William J. Federer. Where, as an example, he cites Oklahoma law in the year 1910, three years after statehood, thus:

If any person shall utter or speak any obscene or lascivious language or word in any public place, or in the presence of females, or in the presence of children under ten (10) years of age, he shall be liable to a fine of not more than One Hundred Dollars ($100.00), or imprisonment for not more than thirty (30) days, or both. Historical Data R.L. 1910, § 2398.

Can you imagine the value of $100.00 in the year 1910?

Can you imagine a jail sentence of 30 days for saying "damn" in a public place?

Can you imagine the impossibility of enacting such a law today?

Does that sound extreme? Note that when the motion picture "Gone With the Wind" was produced in 1939, the motion picture code forbade the use of the profane words of "hell" and "damn". But the Motion Picture Association board passed an amendment to the Production Code on November 1, 1939, that forbade use of the words "hell" or "damn" except when their use "shall be essential and required for portrayal, in proper historical context, of any scene or dialogue based upon folklore... or a quotation from a literary work, provided that no such use shall be permitted which is intrinsically objectionable or offends good taste."[2]

This is evidence of the accepted moral attitude in the United States 163 years after becoming an independent nation.

Evidently, without successful opposition, we have allowed even more than the usage of the words hell and damn. It seems that the profane depravity of base, evil human nature is what sells. Those who morally object have not stopped the fall into the maelstrom of godless immorality. And we have continued to support it, because we need our entertainment. Some may feel they have honored God by not going to those movies. But their children see them, and are indoctrinated by them. And even the parents frequently watch them when offered on their home television, or in home video rentals, or adult movies in hotel and motel rooms. But do churches admonish their congregations not to watch or support such death, or advise them to lovingly admonish their children against such evil indoctrination? Do they urge us to guard our minds and souls from these pathways to apostasy? Does your church ever deliver sermons on discernment? Probably not, because they don't want to offend anyone.

We are in desperate need of righteous guidance in this country. Where else should righteous guidance come from but from the pulpit? It has been the church, believing in and proclaiming the name of Jesus Christ that has been the moral guidance for our country from its inception. It has been the church that has called us to righteousness and away from wickedness. It has been the Lord God the Almighty who has blessed us and provided for us success, riches, peace, and prosperity, more than any nation throughout history. It has been our faith in God and our obedience to God that has brought his blessings to this wonderful country. We demanded good guidance and instruction from our churches because we were believers in God. But now the pulpits are silent and refuse to expose wickedness.

There are a few pastors who are brave enough, and committed enough to speak out on issues and practices that are ungodly, deceptive, and destructive. Most will not. Most will keep silent. They must think if they don't speak out, they will be safe. Safe from attack from the outspoken, rude, and sometimes violent lawless ones. After all, Jesus was offensive, and they killed him. John the Baptist was offensive, and they killed him. The apostles were offensive, and they too were killed. Their offense was that they told the truth. It is the truth that is hated. They all spoke the truth in ways that would be considered politically incorrect. America is falling away from its foundation of Christianity. It is our churches that should be giving guidance, but instead, many are using their precious forty minutes a week to make their congregations feel good. The story of Ruth is a beautiful story, but why preach it for the twentieth time, instead of speaking out against the killing of the unborn, and the attacks on God given marriage. Why not warn them of the addiction to pornographic material on the internet. This is a present danger for them and their children. Why not warn them that what was once a broadcast of the news, has become, in many cases, no more than political propaganda. Why not encourage them to know their Bible. To read and meditate on God's word, to pray more, and to do what it says, in order to advance the kingdom of God, during the short time we have. The silence from America's churches is appalling, and disheartening.

We were a Christian nation. We might even still be. But we have fallen deeply into the abyss of denying Jesus Christ. If our government is to blame, we elected them. If our court system is to blame, we elected the representatives who chose them, and we failed to vote out the offenders when we had the opportunity to do so. That leaves us. If our churches are to blame, we are the ones who support them, and in some cases, we have the power to choose our own pastor and staff. If not, then we can certainly choose our church. We are to blame. If it is our school systems from preschool through college, we are the ones who have the power to demand curricula which honors our values. We vote by our attendance in colleges, and by electing those to the school boards we are in agreement with, and by diligently weeding out those who violate our principles. It is our responsibility, and only we are to blame if our children and young adults are indoctrinated with views that are spiritually deadly. We did it. We have the ability to teach our own children, from birth with the truth that can save their lives, and the life of our nation, as we are told: "Start children off on the way they should go, and even when they are old they will not turn from it" (Proverbs 22:6). That is indicative of another highly important practice. Do you consider yourself to be a Christian? Then do you regularly read and study God's word in the Bible? Do you do so because you love it, or is it like performing required calisthenics? Or eternally sad, are you like many "Christians" who do not read the Bible because they have no interest in it. We who claim to be Christians, we brought this national condition on ourselves. We did not object to evil, and have not demanded the preaching of the full, whole, and complete word of God in our churches. We have not demanded the practice of godly living in our communities and towns. You might register to vote by a party affiliation, but you should be voting according to your faith in Jesus Christ, and your desire to live in a land that obeys his commands. Not a theocracy, but a democratic republic where we can choose political leaders to make and enforce our laws. This calls for truth and discernment. Being too cowardly to speak up for Christ only condemns us. If you know the Bible, Jesus said. "Whoever acknowledges me before others, I will also acknowledge before my Father in heaven. But whoever disowns me before others, I will disown before my Father in heaven" (Matthew 10:32, 33). This comment in no way cancels salvation by grace, but is an awesome reminder that we will be held accountable for all that we do in our lives on earth.

Concerning America, Alexis De Tocqueville wrote: "... Nevertheless in no country does crime more rarely elude punishment. The reason is that everyone conceives himself to be interested in furnishing evidence of the act committed, and in stopping the delinquent. ... In Europe a criminal is an unhappy being who is struggling for his life against the ministers of justice, whilst the population is merely a spectator of the conflict: in America he is looked upon as an enemy of the human race, and the whole of mankind is against him." [3]

I wish that attitude of the people was still with us today, but cowardice and complacency have replaced the godly attitude of personal responsibility. This change in character has, in my opinion, in large part has been caused by the idolization and glamorization of criminal behavior in Hollywood movies, and in the avoidance of pastors to speak out in condemnation of sin.

Many years ago, it was said: America is great because America is good. If America ever ceases to be good America will cease to be great. That goodness of America, which is an indisputable historical fact, was not a self-righteousness, but a faith in the Lord God Almighty, and Jesus Christ his only son who came to earth as a man, and *that* was the foundation upon which this country was established, and *that* is the reason America was good.

In the late 1940s, we had the introduction of television. It was expensive at first, so only a few homes owned one. The available programming was also extremely limited. At first, there was only one channel. At least that is the way it was in my small hometown. Turn on your television in the morning or afternoon, and all you were able to see was a lot of electronic static, referred to as snow. And then, late in the day there was a test pattern. Wow! How interesting. There were probably hours spent watching that static filled test pattern. Finally, in the evening came programming. The acceptance of television came rapidly. Prices for television sets came down, programming options increased, and it was seen as the biggest advancement in advertising ever. We were delighted to own one of these marvelous inventions. We were proud. It dominated our home life, and conversation. Did you see …? Our family closeness and conversation at mealtime was replaced with TV trays, and frozen TV dinners. Instead of talking with each other as a family, we said sssh! I want to hear this commercial.

In the 1940s, programming was family friendly. Programs ranged from *Texaco Star Theater*, and *Howdy Doody*, with Buffalo Bob Smith, to *Kraft Television Theater*, and Ed Sullivan's *Toast of the Town*. These were always moral, even to having a spoken encouragement to kids who watched telling them to be good citizens. In the 1950s we had the news that was friendly and believable from Huntley and Brinkley, and the all too perfect family program *Leave it to Beaver*. Law and order, respect for God and Country, and for family, and neighbors was the standard. In most homes, children were disciplined to guide them to be honest, kind, respectful, truthful, and fair. Foul language was never permitted.

Now that television was accepted and widespread, the encroachment of undesirable elements of profanity and sexual expression, and violence, which had been allowed in some movies, was now coming indiscriminately into each and every home. Like in the motion pictures, actors and actresses we admired, seemed to constantly smoke cigarettes and drink alcohol, and frequently be involved in adultery and divorce. You might say, that's like the real world, but I believe that the real world has gotten much worse because of this endless indoctrination and suggestion. They made it appear that everyone should do it. This too is an example of the power of influence that television had, and still has.

I don't recall anyone speaking out against it. Not even the church that should have been warning us against it and reminding us that a slow acting poison, taken in small doses, is deadly. Maybe it was too subtle, for the church to notice, as it was too subtle for us to notice, but I do remember an analogy telling of a frog, that when placed in boiling water, would jump out, but when placed in cold water would not jump out, even when the water was slowly heated up to the point that it killed the frog. We have stayed in the water too long. With God's help, it's time to jump out. TV is like many other things in life. It can be used for good, or it can be used for evil. We have been all too eager to be entertained, or enthralled, to be critical. In order to see something interesting, we are willing to overlook much that makes us ill. That is a bad decision.

Television started with only a handful of programs. Today, it has many 24-hour news channels, countless 24-hour movie channels, hundreds and hundreds of channels on 24 hours a day. Televised sports have made some people sports fanatics. We need to answer the question, how is my life improved when my team wins? How am I injured when they lose? I enjoy sports, but no sport or any other television programming should be allowed to steal from you your most valuable allotment of time.

It is my opinion that television has been the prime mover in establishing the ethics, mores, beliefs, and personal relationships, in this country. The job that was once the realm of the family and the church. What hope do we have of not being held accountable for the bad choices we have made? What chance do we have from the individual to the nation to ever be in the full light and love of God our savior? For Christians reading this book, the answer is obvious. Read the directions. That is to say, read your Bible. Think about it. Meditate upon it. Read the Psalms and Proverbs for the instruction of your attitude. Read the Gospels, Matthew, Mark, Luke, and John, to know and believe in Jesus. Return to God and he will return to you. Read your Bible. Know your Bible. Talk with God. Pray for guidance and for God's intervention. Revival begins with you and all of those you have contact with.

Chapter 2

Salvation

The Most Important

The only true value in being alive, is to receive eternal life in heaven.

According to the Bible, we live in the flesh, on earth, for a short period of time of about 120 years, or probably less. Is that such a long and valuable time that we should grasp it, and give to it an absolute value? Just imagine, choosing to have faith in Jesus Christ, and because of your faith, being given eternal life where there is no want, no death, no suffering, but in the presence of God who is life, love, acceptance, light, joy, and fulfillment.

Life in this world is short and eternity is forever. To live only for your pleasure and security in this life, and to lose eternity would be the greatest mistake anyone could make. Therefore, this topic of Salvation is the most important item in your life.

Probably the best known verse in the Bible is "For God so loved the world that he gave his one and only Son, that whoever believes in him shall not perish but have eternal life" (John 3:16). This is salvation. This is being saved, believing in Jesus.

That raises a few questions. What does it mean to believe? Even if you want to be saved, why should you look to Jesus? And finally, what is it that you should want to be saved from?

First: What does it mean to believe. A simple question that may have some surprising pitfalls. The primary pitfall is knowledge instead of faith. You might know that Jesus was crucified to pay for the sin of the world, but does that knowledge change your life? Do you find that your preferences have changed because of this knowledge? Do you turn from sin because of your belief in Jesus? Do you ask him for forgiveness when you fail? If so, that's a good start, in fact, if you are making changes to improve your life because of your knowledge of Jesus Christ, that is evidence of faith. Asking him for forgiveness is the sign of repentance. In the gospel of Mark, Jesus says: "The kingdom of God has come near. Repent and believe the good news!" (Mark 1:15). Repent of what? Repent of the times you have broken the law of the Almighty. Breaking God's law is called sin. And how do we know what God's law is? First, he gave you a conscience to help you make moral and ethical decisions.

Then he has actually given the written law, the ten commandments to Moses, followed by many more specific precepts.

The law that God has given us is not a restrictive jail, but rather an owner's manual which explains to us how to get the most out of life.

Psalms 19:7-11

The law of the Lord is perfect,
refreshing the soul.
The statutes of the Lord are
trustworthy,
making wise the simple.
The precepts of the Lord are right,
giving joy to the heart.
The commands of the Lord are radiant,
giving light to the eyes.
The fear of the Lord is pure, enduring forever.
The decrees of the Lord are firm,
and all of them are righteous.
They are more precious than gold,
than much pure gold;
they are sweeter than honey,
than honey from the honeycomb.
By them is your servant warned;
in keeping them there is great reward.

The law of our God is different than other codes of conduct, in fact there are times when only God himself knows that we have violated his law. God's law does not just prohibit evil actions, which we all can see, but he prohibits the evil of the heart, and of the mind. The eighth commandment: "You shall not steal" (Exodus 20:15), an obvious act. And the tenth commandment: "You shall not covet your neighbor's house. You shall not covet your neighbor's wife, or his male or female servant, his ox or donkey, or anything that belongs to your neighbor" (Exodus 20:17). So, God's law is against the act of stealing, which we can see, and against the coveting of anything belonging to your neighbor which is the desire to have (steal) someone else's property. This is something we cannot observe. But only God knows your heart and your motives. "For the word of God is alive and active. Sharper than any double-edged sword, it penetrates even to dividing soul and spirit, joints and marrow; it judges the thoughts and attitudes of the heart. Nothing in all creation is hidden from God's sight. Everything is uncovered and laid bare before the eyes of him to whom we must give account" (Hebrews 4:12). Your secret desires and plans are known completely to the Almighty. Here is one for most of us men. "You have heard that it was said, 'You shall not commit adultery.' But I tell you that anyone who looks at a woman lustfully has already committed adultery with her in his heart" (Matthew 5:27, 28). It is only the Almighty God who gives this law, and only he who knows when it is broken. Do not feel that you alone are guilty. "For all have sinned and fall short of the glory of God" (Romans 3:23), this is why all of us need a savior. We all have sinned.

If you believe in Christ, you will obey him. Speaking of Jesus, it is written: "He became the source of eternal salvation for all who obey him" (Hebrews 5:9). True belief means to obey his commands. "We know that we have come to know him if we keep his commands. Whoever says, 'I know him,' but does not do what he commands is a liar, and the truth is not in that person" (1 John 2:3, 4). "And to whom did God swear that they would never enter his rest if not to those who disobeyed? So, we see that they were not able to enter, because of their unbelief" (Hebrews 3:18, 19). Obeying God is faith in God. Disobeying is unbelief.

Wait a minute. If believing in Jesus, (John 3:16) brings eternal life (salvation), then what's all this stuff about repenting and obeying the law? That is specifically what differentiates between knowledge of God, and faith in God. To obey Jesus, is to believe in him. If on the other hand, you do not obey the commands of Jesus, you obviously do not believe that he is God, and you do not believe that he will judge you for the disposition of your soul. If you do not obey God, then you do not believe that he is God. To obey God is faith, and to not obey is absence of faith, which is unbelief. Faith in Jesus that makes no change in your life, is imaginary. To believe in Jesus is faith in God. From the very start of the Bible, we read about Jesus. In "In the beginning God created the heavens

27

and the earth" (Genesis 1:1). "And God said, 'Let there be light'" (Genesis 1:3). It was this Word of God that created the light. "Now the earth was formless and empty, darkness was over the surface of the deep, and the Spirit of God was hovering over the waters" (Genesis 1:2). In these three verses we see the Trinity. Our triune God. One God, in three persons. God, referred to in Genesis 1:1 is the Hebrew word Elohim, which is a plural noun, but also is singular in meaning when it refers to the one God. God in his triune nature (being) is shown in these scriptures by the almighty God commanding, his Word doing the actual creating, and his Spirit hovering over.

"In the beginning was the Word, and the Word was with God, and the Word was God. He was with God in the beginning. Through him all things were made; without him nothing was made that has been made. In him was life, and that life was the light of all mankind. The light shines in the darkness, but the darkness has not overcome it" (John 1:1-5). This "Word" is the preincarnate Jesus.

"The Word became flesh and made his dwelling among us. We have seen his glory, the glory of the one and only Son, who came from the Father, full of grace and truth." (John 1:14)

In Colossians we read of the God of our creation (Jesus). "The Son is the image of the invisible God, the first born over all creation. For in him all things were created: things in heaven and on earth, visible and invisible, whether thrones or powers or rulers or authorities; all things have been created through him and for him. He is before all things, and in him all things hold together. And he is the head of the body, the church; he is the beginning and the firstborn from among the dead, so that in everything he might have the supremacy. For God was pleased to have all his fullness dwell in him, and through him to reconcile to himself all things, whether things on earth or things in heaven, by making peace through his blood, shed on the cross" (Colossians 1:15-20).

"In your relationships with one another, have the same mindset as Christ Jesus: Who, being in very nature God, did not consider equality with God something to be used to his own advantage; rather, he made himself nothing by taking the very nature of a servant, being made in human likeness. And being found in appearance as a man, he humbled himself by becoming obedient to death – even death on a cross! Therefore God exalted him to the highest place and gave him the name that is above every name, that at the name of Jesus every knee should bow, in heaven and on earth and under the earth, and every tongue acknowledge that Jesus Christ is Lord, to the glory of God the Father" (Philippians 2:5-11).

"Salvation is found in no one else, for there is no other name under heaven given to mankind by which we must be saved" (Acts 4:12).

This is why we look to Jesus to be saved. He was God with us, who as Jesus, overcame death. By the historical record he was witnessed to die on the cross, be buried in the tomb of Joseph of Arimathea, and on the third day rise from the dead. His tomb is empty. He was seen and touched by his disciples. He talked and ate with them. After his resurrection he was seen by hundreds of people over a period of forty days. He was God incarnate, and now is God and with God in heaven. About 700 years before the birth of Christ it is said in Isaiah, "Therefore the Lord himself will give you a sign: The virgin will conceive and give birth to a son, and will call him Immanuel"
(Isaiah 7:14). The name or title Immanuel means: God with us. "Jesus said to her, 'I am the resurrection and the life. The one who believes in me will live even though they die; and whoever lives by believing in me will never die'" (John 11:25, 26).

Now that is Awesome!

When in a science class in college, in the early 1950s, my professor explained that the universe was steady-state. This was the prevailing and accepted theory of the time. The universe has always existed, and always will exist. Matter can neither be created nor destroyed. It wasn't until the 1960s, that Robert Wilson and Arno Penzias discovered the background noise from what is now referred to as the "Big Bang". And now we have "scientific proof" that the universe came into existence at a point in time. Just like God told us thousands of years ago in Genesis 1:1. Science seems to think creation of the universe came from nothing, but the Bible says it was created by the eternal God. Our God who is spirit and who exists eternally, through time, but not bound by our concept of time.

Back to the process of salvation.

One of the earliest claims that Jesus made of his divinity was when he was twelve years old and had been left behind in Jerusalem by Joseph and Mary. When they returned and searched for him, they found him in the temple. "Why were you searching for me?" he asked. "Didn't you know I had to be in my Father's house?" (Luke 2:49). He certainly is not referring to the house of Joseph, his earthly or legal father, but to his true heavenly father, the Lord God Almighty. Jehovah.

It is our sinless Jesus who gave his life for you, that your debt to God, for all of your sins, for which you could not pay, was fully paid, by his sacrificial death on Calvary's cross. "For it is by grace you have been saved, through faith – and this not from yourselves, it is the gift of God – not by works, so that no one can boast" (Ephesians 2:8). We have been saved by the grace of God, through the exercise of our faith in Jesus Christ. This faith we have is also a gift of God.

We are not saved by works. We have no right to heaven because we have been "good". Not because we have done good works, not because we are better than others. We cannot earn heaven. It is a gift by the grace of God, to all who believe in Jesus, John 3:16, and "If you declare with your mouth, 'Jesus is Lord,' and believe in your heart that God raised him from the dead, you will be saved" (Romans 10:9). Therefore, the works mentioned before are not for salvation, but rather as evidence of our faith in Christ, which brings the grace of God. In a few paragraphs you will see an example of the thief who was crucified along with Jesus, who found salvation by faith.

"No one can come to me unless the Father who sent me draws them" (John 6:44). When we come to Jesus, it is because God himself has drawn us to him. "This is why I told you that no one can come to me unless the Father has enabled them" (John 6:65). God must also enable us by giving us the faith we need to believe.

So, it is the Lord God, the Almighty who by his grace, draws us to Jesus, and then by his grace, he gives us the faith we need to believe and be saved. It is grace. The grace of God who gives to us that which is the most valuable, and that which we could in no way get for ourselves. All this through our faith in Jesus Christ who himself has proclaimed "I am the way and the truth and the life. No one comes to the Father except through me" (John 14:6). Faith is the victory! It is this faith in Jesus Christ that saves us. What if you feel left out? What if you have no faith? Be of good cheer, all is not lost. "Consequently, faith comes from hearing the message, and the message is heard through the word about Christ" (Romans 10:17). Therefore, if you lack faith, go to the word of Christ. It is through hearing, or reading the Bible about Jesus, and his words to you, that God himself will give you the faith to believe. I am a scientist, by nature and by schooling. I don't believe the Bible because it promises me eternal life. I believe the Bible because it's true.

An example of salvation is given with the thief on the cross, being crucified with Jesus. The thief finally believed that Jesus was the Christ and he asked Jesus to: "… remember me when you come into your kingdom." Jesus answered him, "Truly I tell you, today you will be with me in paradise" (Luke 23:42, 43). Does this sound too simple? Consider: "And everyone who calls on the name of the Lord will be saved" (Acts 2:21). Some say this thief had no time to do any good works, as a sign of his repentance. The truth is he did two things. First, he believed in Jesus. "Then they ask him, 'What must we do to do the works God requires?' Jesus answered, 'The work of God is this: to believe in the one he has sent'" (John 6:28, 29). Sufficient. Secondly, he made a public confession of his faith. Outstanding! We don't know the eternal fate of most people, even "good" people, but this man is in heaven.

Saved? What are we saved from? We are saved from the lake of fire and burning sulfur, which is the second death. "Then death and Hades were thrown into the lake of fire. The lake of fire is the second death"

(Revelation 20:14). According to the Bible, there are two deaths. The first death is when our bodies stop functioning. Our heart stops, our breathing stops, our brain stops and dies, and we are pronounced (legally) dead. The Bible calls this the first death, and frequently refers to it as "sleep", because from this first death, everyone who dies will be awakened and raised from the dead, for one destination or another.

The second death was designed for the devil and his angels: "Depart from me, you who are cursed, into the eternal fire prepared for the devil and his angels" (Matthew 25:41). For an idea of what this lake of fire, the second death is like: "And the devil, who deceived them, was thrown into the lake of burning sulfur, where the beast and the false prophet had been thrown. They will be tormented day and night forever and ever" (Revelation 20:10). Not a good place to go, and not a destination anyone should be willing to risk by denying the love of God, given to us through the love, life, and sacrificial death of Jesus Christ. "Greater love has no one than this: to lay down one's life for one's friends" (John 15:13).

Whenever salvation and eternal life in heaven have been spoken of, there have been critics and skeptics who confidently proclaim, I don't want to be saved. I'm happy the way I am. If there is anything I don't want, it's the presence of God. I want to be free from a god who tells me what I can or can't do. I will do as I please and I don't need or want your god. How sad. What they believe to be their pleasures, will only last for a short time, and then they will die. After this death is the judgment. "Just as people are destined to die once, and after that to face judgment" (Hebrews 9:27). The judgment for those who have rejected Jesus is the second death, which is the lake of fire and burning sulfur. That deadly and terminal decision was made by them without knowing the attributes of God, from which, they in their ignorance, have declared they wanted to be free. Those beautiful and true attributes of almighty God are described as the fruit of the Spirit: "But the fruit of the spirit is love, joy, peace, forbearance, kindness, goodness, faithfulness, gentleness, and self-control" (Galatians 5:22). How can a person live in the absence of these most beautiful and essential characteristics? No one who knew what these true attributes of God were could ever say, they wanted no part of the one who these words describe. Do you really want to be forever without love? To never have the joy of peace, patience, kindness, or gentleness in your life? Besides the missing out on this beauty and peace on earth, they face the second death. People can only make wise decisions, if they fully understand the choices.

How great is the value of this salvation?

"What good will it be for someone to gain the whole world, yet forfeit their soul?" (Matthew 16:26).
Just imagine, in God's evaluation, your single, solitary soul has more value than the whole world. "Eye has not seen,

nor ear heard, nor have entered into the heart of man the things which God has prepared for those who love Him" (1 Corinthians 2:9 NKJV).

Since salvation is by grace through faith, then let's examine faith. First, faith in God, the creator of all things, is natural. "For since the creation of the world God's invisible qualities – his eternal power and divine nature – have been clearly seen, being understood from what has been made, so that men are without excuse" (Romans 1:20). No rational person can disagree that a Swiss watch, with its gold, engraved case, it's white enameled face, its black filigreed hands, it's finely made gears and cogs, springs and jeweled movement, was created by a creator. Not just created, but created by an exact design, and for a particular purpose. No one can disagree. Then to say that human life on this planet just happened is not intellectually sound, it is dishonest. To examine the intricacies of a single human life, the functioning of the body with bone and muscle, skin and blood, heart and lungs, the ability to see, hear, feel, taste, smell, experience our emotions, and even more amazing, a brain that can remember the past, plan for the future, think, calculate, and even more wonderful, to be able to hear and understand how God has revealed himself to us and given Jesus that we might have life eternal. This is infinitely more complex than a simple Swiss watch. In the face of such evidence, can anyone honestly claim to believe that we were created by chance, without the exact design of our creator, to an exact plan, and for specific purpose? Therefore, faith in God, our creator and the creator of all things, is natural. Even the beautiful laws of chemistry and physics proclaim the majesty of God our creator. The good news is that faith in God is not a matter of intellect. If it were, only the intelligent people would believe. But faith in God is a matter of honesty. It is available to everyone.

Secondly, although the evidence of God, naturally seen in creation, is available to all, salvation begins with faith in Jesus Christ, and that is not common knowledge. People must hear the words, or read the words of God that tell us of Jesus. This is where witnessing begins. We must tell them. P. T. Barnum, the great showman of the Barnum and Bailey Circus was once criticized for using an excess of advertising. He answered, if you don't tell 'em, they ain't never gonna know. It pays to advertise. At least that is the way I remember it from a book I read on P. T. Barnum's life, many, many decades ago, and that is the way it is today. The great commission that Jesus gave to his disciples is recorded in Matthew 28:18-20 "All authority in heaven and on earth has been given to me. Therefore go and make disciples of all nations, baptizing them in the name of the Father and of the Son and of the Holy Spirit, and teaching them to obey everything I have commanded you. And surely I am with you always, to the very end of the age."

Since we are saved by the grace of God, through faith in Jesus Christ, it is our faith in Jesus that gives us the heart's desire to do good works. Especially to share with others the boundless gift of grace we have received from God. But here is another good reason to live a life of honoring God with witnessing and good works, that is rewards. Some Christians seem to believe that since they believe in Jesus Christ, that they will enter heaven in regal splendor, with the trumpets blowing a magnificent welcome. Well, maybe. Maybe not. All people will be judged by God. Those whose names are not written in the Book of Life, will be cast into the lake of fire and burning Sulfur, which is the second death. Those whose names are written in the Book of Life will be saved. The way to have your name written in the Book of Life, is to be a believer in Jesus Christ. But how about Christians? Those of us whose names *are* written in the Book of Life? We too will stand before the judgment seat of Christ. "For we must all appear before the judgment seat of Christ, so that each of us may receive what is due us for the things done while in the body, whether good or bad" (2 Corinthians 5:10).

In 1 Corinthians 3:10–15 Paul is *only* talking to Christians, we who have the foundation through our faith in Jesus. The works of our lives will be tested in the fire. If we have built on our foundation in Christ with the works of being a good disciple, of sharing the good news, with doing all sorts of good works by living the fruit of the Spirit listed in Galatians chapter 5, by exercising our spiritual gifts, etc. and etc. honoring God, praying prayers which delight God, loving truth and justice, we well be rewarded. But even if all of our works are burned up in the fire, we who believe in Christ <u>still</u> will be saved, because of our faith in Christ Jesus, but saved only as one escaping through the flames.

I don't know how thinly the Lord cuts this "belief in Jesus", but it would seem to me that it would be best to have some evidence. "As the body without the spirit is dead, so faith without deeds is dead" (James 2:26). Still, in talking about the minimal faith needed for salvation, the unsure might take confidence in Acts 2:21: "And everyone who calls on the name of the Lord will be saved" No matter how thin your faith is in Jesus, if it gets you into heaven, even as one escaping through the flames, Hallelujah!

If you were to repent of your sins, and by faith accept Jesus Christ as your savior, you would be saved, but who would notice? "I tell you that in the same way there will be more rejoicing in heaven over one sinner who repents than over ninety-nine righteous persons who do not need to repent" (Luke 15: 7). If you have no faith, get faith. If your faith is weak, strengthen your faith. Listen to the words of Christ being preached, or read his words in the Bible, and faith will come to you. There is a caveat here, some preaching is erroneous, and you need to be a Berean. In Acts 17:11, Paul mentions the Bereans who were of noble character, and they listened to the message with great eagerness, but after listening to the message that Paul preached, they went to the scriptures and read them to make sure that Paul had told them the truth. Whenever we listen to today's preaching, we need to go to the scriptures and see if what we just heard is the truth. The basis of our belief is the Bible. (Our collective beliefs in the principles and truths of God is our religious doctrine.) The Bible is the only written source of truth concerning the Almighty God, how we began, the creation of all things, his relationship to mankind, Jesus, the Word of God, and how we have hope of eternal life through faith in him. It is not our church, or any individual whether family, friend, pastor, priest, or vision. Hopefully all of these sources will be true, but check them out in the only authoritative source, the Bible. Know your Bible. Your life depends on it. Be a Berean!

The error of relying on the knowledge of Jesus, rather than having faith in him is exampled by these words of Jesus: "Not everyone who says to me, 'Lord, Lord', will enter the kingdom of heaven, but only the one who does the will of my Father who is in heaven. Many will say to me on that day, 'Lord, Lord, did we not prophesy in your name and in your name drive out demons and in your name perform many miracles?' Then I will tell them plainly, 'I never knew you. Away from me, you evildoers!'" (Matthew 7:21- 23). Those verses just quoted show the difference between "knowledge of Jesus", and "faith in Jesus". **Knowledge of Jesus only requires knowledge. Saving faith in Jesus requires repentance and obedience.** "If you love Me, keep My commandments" (John 14:15 NKJV). "Why do you call me, 'Lord, Lord' and not do what I say?" (Luke 6:46).

Today, there are some on television, and elsewhere who to me, sound as though they are using the name of Jesus only as a source of income, but I will let God decide about that. Still the examples in Matthew 7:21 just cited, and this following passage seem to be cases of just that. "Some Jews who went around driving out evil spirits tried to invoke the name of the Lord Jesus over those who were demon-possessed. They would say, 'In the name of Jesus, whom Paul preaches, I command you to come out.' Seven sons of Sceva, a Jewish chief priest, were doing this. One day the evil spirit answered them, 'Jesus I know, and Paul I know about, but who are you?' Then the man who had the evil spirit jumped on them and overpowered them all. He gave them such a beating that they ran out of the house naked and bleeding" (Acts 19:13–16).

If you are ever in a place where you are asked: Jesus I know, and Paul I know, but who are you? I hope you will be able to truthfully answer; I am a child of the King, a servant of the Lord God Almighty, through faith in Jesus Christ, my savior.

Question. What is the minimum a person must do to be saved?

The minimum is "Believe on the Lord Jesus Christ and you will be saved" (Acts 16:31). "Everyone who calls on the name of the Lord will be saved" (Romans 10:13). Pardon my being redundant, but these verses and this concept is so basic to the most important item in life, they must be repeated. It is from this base that people can grow in their faith and understanding to be loved, saved, and rewarded by God. Still, it is important to have faith in Jesus Christ, and not just knowledge of Jesus Christ. But even in discussing the possibility of minimal salvation, it seems to require a faith in Jesus in order to call on his name, doesn't it? And if this calling on his name is something you do before your last breath on earth, there must be some belief in him, for your eternal hope. Don't you want to know more about him? Would you not want to thank him and live to please him, and do what he asks? But how many people, calling themselves Christian, and having confidence in their eternal security, don't love him enough to even read his words? Very sad. And I'm sure their disinterest is not without consequence. Examine the following, as an example of a sinner's prayer. A prayer for God to save you.

"Jesus, I am a sinner, and I am sorry. Please forgive my sins and come into my heart as my Lord and Savior. I repent (turn away) form sin and I commit my life to you. I will study your word, follow your teachings, and obey your commands. And Lord, show me what you want me to do; what part I can play in furthering your kingdom. Thank you, Lord, for saving me. In Jesus' name I pray, Amen."

This prayer was printed in the Tulsa Beacon[1], a weekly newspaper of Tulsa, Oklahoma, on April 19, 2018, in a letter to the editor. I was greatly impressed when reading it because it covers the basics that a Christian should believe, and because of belief, the appropriate changes in their life. I am a sinner, I'm sorry. Please forgive me. Come into my innermost being and dwell with me. I commit my life to you. I will study your word; I will obey your commands. Show me how I can live a life which will further your loving plan for people on earth.

How many people, who call themselves Christian, do or even care about these things? I'm asking specifically about the last three.

Since you are a Christian because of your faith in Jesus, and have eternal life given by the grace of God, I pray for you that your time of being judged before the Judgment seat of Christ will be a time of joy.

Remember, sin will not keep you out of heaven. Unbelief will keep you out. Sin can be forgiven.

Directions to Heaven

Chapter 3

Salvation Without Knowledge of Jesus Christ

"Jesus answered, 'I am the way and the truth and the life. No one comes to the Father except through me" (John 14:6).

"For God so loved the world that he gave his one and only Son, that whoever believes in him shall not perish but have eternal life. For God did not send his Son into the world to condemn the world, but to save the world through him. Whoever believes in him is not condemned, but whoever does not believe stands condemned already because they have not believed in the name of God's one and only Son" (John 3:16-18).

"Salvation is found in no one else, for there is no other name under heaven given to mankind by which we must be saved" (Acts 4:12).

Many Christians have wondered about the countless billions of people who have lived and died, without ever hearing the gospel of Jesus Christ, our Lord and Savior. The pastors I have listened to have expressed themselves one way or another, but in conclusion have said, they are not saved, they have no place in heaven, and therefore must be relegated to an eternal state of suffering in the lake of fire, which is the second death. Some Christians who have accepted this conclusion, are still, uncomfortable with it. It does not seem fair. Even so, we know that God is good, he is the only one who is good, and he is just. Everything he does is right and good, even when we cannot understand.

Could it be, that these billions are simply the tares mentioned in Matthew 13:24-30? Instead of tares, some Bible versions refer to them as weeds, or darnel. Darnel is a poisonous grass, resembling wheat. In this parable, Jesus is using the comparison of a worthless weed, to people who seem to be the unsaved who are headed for damnation. Those who will ultimately be cast into the lake of fire. (See Revelation 20:11-15). This weed in its early growth resembles the wheat, and cannot be separated out because doing so would damage the wheat. Therefore, it must be allowed to grow with the wheat until harvest. At the harvest the weeds are bound in bundles and burned. When the wheat and the weeds are compared to people, it would seem the righteous people, represented by the wheat are the saved people, and the unsaved people, represented by the weeds, are burned. In eternal fire? It looks that way. The weeds are sown by the enemy, this is Satan, the devil. The weeds are the *sons* of the evil one. Could this mean that after God's creation of Adam and Eve, that Satan also created people to resemble those created by God, but without a soul? They definitely would not be created in God's image. Adam, and all people from Adam and Eve are made in the image of God, and have body and soul. (See Genesis 2:7) If that were so, that there might be people created by the evil one, who would not have souls that were God breathed, so that God's burning of them might not be an eternal punishment. They possibly would simply parish. On the other hand, if they are creations of Satan, possibly they will suffer with him forever. The Bible does not say that. I only imagine that as a possibility, without scriptural confirmation. What else could these weeds be? They are evidently people who do not have faith in Jesus Christ.

Jesus tells the following parable:

"The Kingdom of heaven is like a man who sowed good seed in his field. But while everyone was sleeping, his enemy came and sowed weeds among the wheat, and went away. When the wheat sprouted and formed heads, then the weeds also appeared.
The owner's servants came to him and said, 'Sir, didn't you sow good seed in your field? Where then did the weeds come from?'
'An enemy did this,' he replied.
'The servants ask him, 'Do you want us to go and pull them up?'
'No,' he answered, 'because while you are pulling the weeds, you may uproot the wheat with them. Let both grow together until the harvest. At that time I will tell the harvesters: First collect the weeds and tie them in bundles

47

to be burned; then gather the wheat and bring it into my barn'" (Matthew 13:24-30).

The disciples of Jesus who heard this parable did not understand it, so Jesus gave them the interpretation.

"The one who sowed the good seed is the Son of Man. The field is the world, and the good seed stands for the people of the kingdom. The weeds are the people of the evil one, and the enemy who sows them is the devil. The harvest is the end of the age, and the harvesters are angels. As the weeds are pulled up and burned in the fire, so it will be at the end of the age. The Son of Man will send out his angels, and they will weed out of his kingdom everything that causes sin and all who do evil. They will throw them into the blazing furnace, where there will be weeping and gnashing of teeth. Then the righteous will shine like the sun in the kingdom of their Father. Whoever has ears, let them hear" (Matthew 13:37-43).

In Matthew 13:38, in the above quotation, different versions of the Bible have used different words to express their translations, as follows:

KJV – the good seed are the children of the kingdom; but the tares are the children of the wicked *one.*

NKJV – the good seeds are the sons of the kingdom, but the tares are the sons of the wicked one.

NASB – and *as for* the good seed, these are the sons of the kingdom; and the tares are the sons of the evil *one*;

NIV – the good seed stands for the people of the kingdom. The weeds are the people of the evil one

The great commission of Christ is, "All authority in heaven and on earth has been given to me. Therefore go and make disciples of all nations, baptizing them in the name of the Father and of the Son and of the Holy Spirit, and teaching them to obey everything I have commanded you. And surely I am with you always, to the very end of the age" (Matthew 28:16-20). I mention the Lord's great commission at this time to remind you that it is the Lord's fervent desire that people of *all* nations be saved. There are no people on earth who are to be excluded from receiving eternal life through faith in Jesus Christ. We therefore cannot automatically write off any group of people, or even any individual.

First, let me make my beliefs perfectly clear. I believe, that without the blood atonement of Jesus Christ, on Cavalry's cross, and his bodily resurrection, there would be no human saved. I mean that no human could have perfect righteousness in heaven, had it not been for the sacrifice of Jesus to pay for their sins. This includes Adam and all who come after him. That list includes Enoch, Elijah, Abraham, Mary, and to shorten the list, everyone. Speaking of Abraham, why did God credit him with righteousness? "Abram believed the Lord, and he credited it to him as righteousness" (Genesis 15:6). So, is Abraham "saved"? Is Enoch in heaven? Of course they are. There is a scripture: "But now apart from the law the righteousness of God has been made known to which the Law and the Prophets testify. This righteousness is given through faith in Jesus Christ to all who believe. There is no difference between Jew and Gentile, for all have sinned and fall short of the glory of God, and all are justified freely by his grace through the redemption that came by Christ Jesus. God presented Christ as a sacrifice of atonement, through the shedding of his blood – to be received by faith. He did this to demonstrate his righteousness, because in his forbearance he had left the sins committed beforehand unpunished ..." (Romans 3:21-25). I believe it is this: **"in his forbearance he had left the sins committed beforehand unpunished"** that has allowed an early entrance into heaven for Enoch, and others, but the completion of their righteousness could only be through the atonement of Jesus Christ. Adam, and all people after him are tainted by Adam's sin. This is a common Christian doctrinal belief. Redemption is through Christ and Christ alone, and it comes by way of faith. Was Abram a sinful man? We know that he was, yet God gave him the credit of righteousness, because of his faith. It seems imperative that Abram's sin committed beforehand, must have been left unpunished until it was atoned for by Jesus Christ.

It is Christian doctrine that salvation comes by the grace of God, through faith in Jesus Christ, from Ephesians chapter 2. Many times pastors have explained that knowledge of Jesus is not sufficient. True faith is necessary. True faith that leads to repentance of sin, and a desire and effort to please and obey God. No one can define exactly how much faith is necessary, or how to recognize it. We can think that a person is a believer in and a follower of Jesus by their words and deeds, but only God knows the heart, which gets me back to those billions of people who have never heard the gospel of Jesus. If Abram can be declared righteous by God, because of his faith, is it possible for someone else to receive righteousness by their faith? Abram did not know God's name? No, but he believed. Since God is all knowing, then he knows everything about everyone who has ever lived. He knows and understands what each person was given and what they had to deal with. Their environment, their intellect, the pressures they encountered, and how and why they responded the way they responded. If the word of God, examines everyone, as is explained by: "**For the word of God is alive and active. Sharper than any double-edged sword, it penetrates even to dividing soul and spirit, joints and marrow; it judges the thoughts and attitudes of the heart. Nothing in all creation is hidden from God's sight. Everything is uncovered and laid bare before the eyes of him to whom we must give account**" (Hebrews 4:12, 13). It would seem obvious that God's perfect understanding of how each person has responded to life, and how each person has responded to the faith that God has given them, is far more accurate than any of our Church doctrines, or our ability to discern whether a person is a believer in Jesus or not. God thoroughly knows and

51

understand each person, their actions and reactions, and ultimately each person's true belief, whether or not that person "believed God" and lived according as they could, or if they did not. I know it is possible, but I also think that it is reasonable that God would do this. Such a person might be recognized at the great white throne judgment of Revelation 20:11–15, which most all pastors proclaim to be a judgment that sends all of those judged to eternal fire. If so, why would the book of life be open there, if everyone at that judgment were to be forever doomed? Could it be that some, who did not know the name of Jesus, and did not know of the name of God, might have had their faith in the true God, and had that faith reckoned to them as righteousness, the same way that Abram's faith was in Genesis 15:6? Even if this were to have happened, they might be saved because of their faith, but they would still need the righteousness offered by the gift of Jesus Christ, the full payment for their sin. And, to the best of my knowledge, they have not been given a covenant land, and the promise to become a great nation, so they would differ from Abraham. Even if this is done, this is not a doctrinal idea to give confidence to anyone, especially not to anyone who has heard and rejected the gospel of Jesus Christ. This is not a Biblical concept, but in my mind it is only a thought which recognizes God's absolute knowledge, authority, and his unfailing justice.

The image sometimes held of God is that he is a white-haired old gentleman who has unlimited power and all knowledge, and the ability to be everywhere at once.

That seems to fall a bit short of reality. In my opinion, every deed that anyone has done, every thought that any human has ever had, along with all other information is something that God is constantly aware of. He is aware of each and every electron, neutrino, all named and unnamed subatomic particles, where they came from, and where they are going. He is continually aware of the origin and pathway of every photon of light throughout all the estimated two trillion galaxies, and everything else within and everything beyond the limits of the universe. He is God and there is no other. God is aware of things we humans are not aware of like spirits, powers, and principalities. God brought them into existence and he is constantly and thoroughly aware of them and has absolute authority and control over them. God is always and forever aware of everything, and has absolute authority over everything. He is not a man, He is God.

"Before me no god was formed, nor will there be one after me" (Isaiah 43:10).

"I am the first and I am the last; apart from me there is no God" (Isaiah 44:6).

"I am the Alpha and the Omega," says the Lord God, "who is, and who was, and who is to come, the Almighty" (Revelation 1:8).

"Holy, holy, holy is the Lord God Almighty, who was, and is, and is to come" (Revelation 4:8). Amen!

Directions to Heaven

Chapter 4

Human Understanding

The reason the Word of God, who created everything that is, had to come to earth as Jesus, born of the virgin Mary, live as a sinless God/man, then give his life's blood as a sacrifice on Calvary's cross, for atonement for sin, so that God the Father, would be satisfied that sufficient payment had been made to pay for the sins of the whole world, is, in my opinion, incomprehensible. Many times I have heard preachers explain why this was necessary, but in my own mind, as a simple human, I find it to be beyond human understanding.

We who live on earth, in our ignorance, place so little value on life, that we kill one another. We in our arrogant ignorance can start wars, for personal gain. If we try to answer the question why Jesus would do what he did for us, we can only suspect a human answer. But in God's evaluation we read: "What good will it be for someone to gain the whole world, yet forfeit their soul? Or what can anyone give in exchange for their soul?" (Matthew 16:26). The whole world has not enough value to equal the value of one soul. This was said by Jesus to his disciples, in terms that they could grasp. What I now believe is that the value of one, single human soul, that is granted life eternal, in the presence of the Lord God, has more value than the entirety of all creation, and infinitely more. The reason we can't see why Jesus would pay such a price, could be because we cannot calculate, or even come close to imagining, the value that we people, who are created in the image of God truly have. Each one of us. From conception to the grave, and eternally beyond. "For those who are led by the Spirit of God are the children of God. The Spirit you received does not make you slaves, so that you live in fear again; rather, the Spirit you received brought about your adoption to sonship. And by him we cry, 'Abba, Father.' The Spirit himself testifies with our spirit that we are God's children. Now if we are children, then we are heirs – heirs of God and co-heirs with Christ, if indeed we share in his sufferings in order that we may also share in his glory" (Romans 8:14-17). Now what do you think is the value, of being "co-heir with Christ"?

"And without the shedding of blood there is no forgiveness" (Hebrews 9:22). Why is the shedding of blood necessary for the remission of sin? This is another matter that is outside of the realm of human understanding. We know of this from Genesis 3:21 that the Lord shed blood, because of Adam's sin. God made garments of skin for Adam and Eve to cover their nakedness, which they became aware of because of their sin. Garments of skin cannot be made without the shedding of blood. The blood sacrifices in Old Testament times were temporal examples.

The shedding of the blood of Jesus is the eternal example. We are told: "For the life of a creature is in the blood, and I have given it to you to make atonement for yourselves on the altar; it is the blood that makes atonement for one's life" (Leviticus 17:11). That was God's command at that time, in preparing for the final sacrifice.

In the words of Jesus: "First he said, 'Sacrifices and offerings, burnt offerings and sin offerings you did not desire, nor were you pleased with them' – though they were offered in accordance with the law. Then he said, 'Here I am, I have come to do your will.' He sets aside the first to establish the second. And by that will, we have been made holy through the sacrifice of the body of Jesus Christ once for all.

Day after day every priest stands and performs his religious duties; again and again he offers the same sacrifices, which can never take away sins. But when this priest had offered for all time one sacrifice for sins, he sat down at the right hand of God, and since that time he waits for his enemies to be made his footstool. For by one sacrifice he has made perfect forever those who are being made holy" (Hebrews 10:8-14).

Once again, this can be believed because God has revealed it to us, but it cannot be reasoned out by human understanding. Thus the Lord has declared: "As the heavens are higher than the earth, so are my ways higher than your ways and my thoughts than your thoughts" (Isaiah 55:9).

The life is in the blood, and certainly we know that the only true value that we have, is life.

The Lord our God is a triune God. A singular God in three persons, known as God the Father, God the Son, and God the Holy Spirit. It is because of this threefold revealing of God, that we use the human term, Trinity. Many people have explained how God exists in three persons, but once again, in my opinion, this is not within human understanding. We can see in nature, the clover, which has three leaves, although some think a four-leaf clover is lucky. It is still one clover. We can see things like water which can exist as liquid, or solid when frozen, or as gas when in the form of water vapor. But water is only a physical chemical compound. One of the realities that intrigued me in physics, was the duality of light. Our professor finally stated, "If someone should ever ask you: "Is light composed of waves, or is light composed of particles?", you should answer, yes, definitely. Singular light is in waves and at the same time it is in particles (photons). Both of those forms are light. None of these things can explain our triune God. The terms that God himself has used to define himself are sufficient, even though God himself is far beyond human understanding.

Why should we have faith in such things that are not humanly understandable? I have faith to believe that the

Bible is true and that it is the word of God. This faith has come through many years of reading, meditating on, and teaching the Bible. Faith comes from hearing, reading, and understanding the words in the Bible. The words that tell us that God created all that is, and how God has responded to humans, from Adam, to Abraham, to you. The Bible has been proven true in many ways, but on a scientific basis, proof can be irrefutably made with a study of fulfilled prophecy. I do not believe in psychics, soothsayers, fortune tellers, or horoscopes, I have more common sense than that. But how could God's prophets be able to foretell and specifically describe many, many future events by years and hundreds of years, with great accuracy, if that knowledge were not given to them by the all knowing God from whom they say their prophecies have come? There are many books on the hundreds and hundreds of Bible prophecies, of which: *Every Prophecy of the Bible* by John F. Walvoord[1] is a good one. Amazingly there are hundreds of prophecies that have been fulfilled, and many still in progress, and many still in the future. The Bible is true. In the Bible, I believe the things I do not understand, because of my absolute belief in the things I do understand.

I believe in God through seeing his creation. I believe in Jesus, the Word of God, who from the beginning was and always has been God. I believe he lived on earth as a man, because of the overwhelming evidence. I even decided that I would believe in the word of God, even if there were no God, because it is true. What he declares to be good is good, and what he calls evil, is evil. "Your word is a lamp for my feet, a light on my path" (Psalm 119:105). His words are beautiful and true. However, I also approach life with a scientific attitude, therefore, I look to see if there is additional proof.

The Bible has been proven true by its recorded history, which has been proven many times through non-biblical records and through many archaeological discoveries. Additional evidence is given in the writings of non-Christian historians who have substantiated Jesus and the Christians who believed in him. Josephus was one of the more prolific writers, but also many others like: Pliny the governor of Bithynia in Turkey, Tacitus, Thallus, and Lucian. Josephus spoke of Jesus being seen after his resurrection, some of the other writers mostly mentioned the Christians who were persecuted for their belief Jesus.

The prophecies of Jesus from the Old Testament are astounding. The following are only a couple of prophetic examples, neither of which is an exhaustive account.

In the eighth century BC, the minor prophet Micah prophesied the birth of the messiah was to be in Bethlehem Ephrathah, recorded in Micah chapter 5 verse 2. While Joseph and Mary were living in Nazareth in Galilee, and Mary was nine months pregnant, Caesar Augustus just happened to issue a decree that ordered Joseph to go to his own town to register for the census. When Joseph and Mary went to Bethlehem to register, Jesus was born in Bethlehem, just as it was prophesied 700 years earlier.

The description of the crucifixion of Jesus can be found in the following Bible books and chapters: Matthew chapter 27, Mark chapter 15, Luke chapter 23, and John chapter 19. First read these accounts, then read Psalms 22, this description of his crucifixion that was written about 1000 years before it happened, and about 500 years before the practice of crucifixion had first been used. Then read Isaiah chapter 53, that was written 700 years BC. Amazing!

There are countless (to me) prophecies about other people. One of these is the prophecy of Cyrus, that is found in Isaiah chapter 44 and verses 24–28. This prophecy was fulfilled 300 years later in the 5th century BC, as recorded in the Book of Ezra, chapter 1. This prophecy, calling Cyrus by name, as the one who allowed the Jews to rebuild the temple, was made 150 years before Cyrus was born. That's more accurate than the weekly weather report.

Other thoughts

The Star

I do not think that the star of Bethlehem is prophesied in the Bible. I don't know how the wise men, Magi from the east, knew the star was to guide them to the one who had been born king of the Jews. Possibly form the writings in the Old Testament, or more likely they received the information in a dream or vision that had come to them from God. They saw the star, when it rose, but did everyone see it? I don't think so. There did not seem to be a general arousal because of it. King Herod and his wise men did not seem to be aware of it. I think, only the Magi saw it. Also, it was not stationary, it moved. It was not a star in the heavens, or an arrangement of planets, but some light, especially created by God that was closer to the earth. After guiding the Magi to Jerusalem, it must have vanished from sight, because they asked, "Where is the one who has been born king of the Jews? We saw his star when it rose and have come to worship him" (Matthew 2:2). After leaving King Herod the Magi once again saw the same star. This time it moved before them until it stopped over the exact place where Jesus was. This guidance could not have from a star, light years away in the sky, but a local light that guided them precisely to one house. The story of this star is only found in chapter 2 of the gospel of Matthew.

The Jews at the time of Jesus

I have heard that the Jews have been given a high intelligence by God, and see no reason to doubt that. When Jesus came, they were expecting a Messiah who would "save them from their enemies". They rejected Jesus, because he certainly was no military conqueror. They seemed to be expecting a general, from God who would defeat all the countries that oppressed them, like a football coach who would have a winning season against all other teams. Then they would march down the street with the banner: "We're Number One".

Jesus was their Messiah who came to defeat their enemies, but their enemies were not Rome, and other countries. Their enemies then, were the same as their enemies are today. Their enemies are sin and death.

Directions to Heaven

Chapter 5

The Rapture

There is a most spectacular event that is going to take place in the very near future.

If you participate in this event, your joyous eternity is assured.

Here is what is going to happen. The Lord Jesus Christ will come down from heaven, not all the way to the earth, but up in the sky and in the clouds above the earth, and then he will take up to be with him, all the people who are believers in him who have died. Then, all of us who are believers in him who are still living, will also be caught up into the air to be with him forever.

Any questions?

"For the Lord himself will come down from heaven, with a loud command, with the voice of the archangel and with the trumpet call of God, and the dead in Christ will rise first. After that, we who are still alive and are left will be caught up together with them in the clouds to meet the

Lord in the air. And so we will be with the Lord forever. Therefore encourage each other with these words" (1 Thessalonians 4:16-18).

The scripture says that we will be 'caught up'. The Greek word used was harpazo which has the meaning of caught away, or snatched away rapidly, by force. Rapture has the meaning of extreme pleasure, and the archaic meaning: The act of carrying off.

You don't have to worry about what you are wearing, or the condition of your body. In that instant, we all will be changed. "Listen, I will tell you a mystery: We will not all sleep, but we will all be changed — in a flash, in the twinkling of an eye, at the last trumpet. For the trumpet will sound, the dead will be raised imperishable, and we will be changed. For the perishable must clothe itself with the imperishable, and the mortal with immortality. When the perishable has been clothed with the imperishable, and the mortal with immortality, then the saying that is written will come true: "Death has been swallowed up in victory." "Where, O death, is your victory? Where, O death, is your sting?" (1 Corinthians 15:51-57). I believe that this could be the fulfillment of: "Dear friends, now we are children of God, and what we will be has not yet been made known. But we know that when he appears, we shall be like him, for we shall see him as he is" (1 John 3:2). So, when we meet the Lord in the air, at the rapture, it will not be our mortal and perishable bodies that go sailing up, but rather our changed, and now imperishable and immortal bodies. Our physical, perishable bodies might remain, so that those left on earth could believe that we died, but maybe not, since the tomb of Jesus is empty. It could be that when our mortal bodies are changed into the immortal, nothing will be left. How about people who have been cremated? What about lives lost at sea, whose bodies have had thousands of years to disintegrate? Or the saints of the Lord whose bodies were burned at the stake? Since it is only the perishable body that has been lost, the soul (the life that God breathed into Adams nostrils, and has given to each of us) remains intact. This life is sometimes referred to as the soul, or as the spirit. The soul of a person is not damaged when a person loses a hand, or a leg, or is blind. The soul is intact. When we exchange the perishable for the imperishable, isn't this to be our eternal body? Since it is our new and imperishable body, not our old mortal and perishable body then it will have no missing parts, or non-functioning parts. It seems that there will be personal identity. When Moses and Elijah appeared before Peter, James, and John, on the mountain where the transfiguration took place, they were recognizable. Jesus could be recognized in his resurrection body. It seems reasonable that our imperishable bodies will be perfect in every respect.

Several books and movies have tried to paint a picture of what life on earth will be like, after all Christians are removed from the earth by this catching up, this rapture of all believers in Christ. Unfortunately, for those left behind, they will not only be missing the good influence of the kind, true, and godly people who had faith in Jesus, but also taken out of the way will be the Holy Spirit of God. It is the Holy Spirit who even now is restraining evil in the world. After the rapture, there will be a time known as "the great tribulation". It will be the most horrible time the world has ever known. This is how Jesus referred to it: "For then there will be great distress, unequaled from the beginning of the world until now — and never to be equaled again" (Matthew 24:21). Think of history. Think of the horrible times. Think of the unspeakable deeds that have been done to people. The time of the tribulation will be desperately worse. A time of unbridled evil. Why do I say unbridled? Because the Holy Spirit of God, who is now holding back evil, and who indwells every believer in Christ, (Acts 1:1-9 and 2:1-4), will be taken out of the way. "For the secret power of lawlessness is already at work; but the one who now holds it back will continue to do so till he is taken out of the way. And then the lawless one will be revealed, whom the Lord Jesus will overthrow with the breath of his mouth and destroy by the splendor of his coming" (2 Thessalonians 2:7, 8). This lawless one is the Antichrist. The Antichrist, is the one who will make a seven year covenant with Israel, (Daniel 9:27). The signing of the seven year covenant, marks the beginning of the last seven years, leading up to the battle of Armageddon, the last war. The end of this war will be the second coming of the Lord Jesus Christ. We don't know when the revealing of the Antichrist will happen. It could be before, during, or after the signing of the seven year covenant. But we do know, that when he is revealed, the Holy Spirit, indwelling each believer will have already been taken out of the way, and that will have been the rapture.

For the people who remain behind, and are not taken up to be with the Lord, you are in for extremely desperate times, however, mark these words, the end for you has not yet come. There are things that you must do, and things that you must not do, if you want to save your soul for eternity. You must **not** worship the Antichrist, or the beast, or the image of the beast. You must **not** accept his name or his number, that is his mark, which will be necessary for people to receive in order to be able to buy and sell. When demanded to take his mark, or worship him, you must refuse and proclaim faith in Jesus Christ. This claim will probably get you killed. If you choose to have faith in Jesus, and call upon his name to save you, your death should be viewed as sweet, because you will have chosen to receive an eternity in heaven, rather than being cast into the lake of fire, eternally. If you chose to have faith in Jesus, you will not be alone. "After this I looked and there before me was a great multitude that no one could count, from every nation, tribe, people and language, standing before the throne and before the Lamb. They were wearing white robes and were holding palm branches in their hands" (Revelation 7:9). "Then one of the elders asked me, 'These in white robes — who are they, and where did they come from?' I answered, 'Sir, you know.' And he said, 'These are they who have come out of the great tribulation, they have washed their robes and made them white in the blood of the Lamb'" (Revelation 7:13, 14). This is a prophecy of an enormous multitude of people, who will have missed the rapture, but still entered heaven. To do this they must have chosen to be martyred for their faith in Jesus Christ, rather than worship the beast or his image, or take his mark. Please do not choose to endure the torture and death of the great tribulation. Accept Jesus now so that you may escape in the rapture.

To see what God foretells us about this period of time of the great tribulation, see Revelation chapters 6 through 19. The explanation is symbolic, but clear enough for you to see what a most horrible time this will be.

If this sounds disturbing to you, at least you have been forewarned. Don't take my word for it, consult the source. Read the Bible and know the Bible. Jesus is your life.

The book of Acts tells about the infusion of the Holy Spirit into all believers on the day of Pentecost. "Do not leave Jerusalem, but wait for the gift my Father promised, which you have heard me speak about. For John baptized with water, but in a few days you will be baptized with the Holy Spirit" (Acts 1:4, 5). This third person of our triune God, is the Advocate, or in some translations is called the Counselor, or the Helper, of whom Jesus spoke, "But very truly I tell you, It is for your good that I am going away. Unless I go away, the Advocate will not come to you; but if I go, I will send him to you. When he comes, he will prove the world to be in the wrong about sin and righteousness and judgment: about sin, because people do not believe in me; about righteousness, because I am going to the Father, where you can see me no longer; and about judgment, because the prince of this world now stands condemned" (John 16:7-11). The Holy Spirit will be taken out of the way before the Antichrist is revealed. See the reference in 2 Thessalonians 2:7,8 quoted earlier. The following tribulation will be a seven year period, divided into two parts of three and one half years each. The term "great tribulation" should be applied only to the second part, or the last three and a half years. The Great Tribulation will start when the world leader, the Antichrist, will break the seven year covenant with Israel, and proclaim himself to be God.

The evil one, the lawless one who rules at this time will be the Antichrist. He has not yet been revealed. Antichrist can mean one opposed to the Lord Christ, or it can mean, the one who claims to be Christ, as he will, during the great tribulation. "He will oppose and will exalt himself over everything that is called God or is worshiped, so that he sets himself up in God's temple, proclaiming himself to be God" (2 Thessalonians 2:4).

The timing we are given here is that the rapture will occur before the Antichrist is revealed. It does not say how long before he is revealed, only that it will be before. There are several events that must happen before Jesus sets up his kingdom on earth, at his second coming, but there is nothing else necessary before the rapture, except the

71

rebellion, the great apostasy, which seems to be occurring now. The rapture could happen at any time.

But if you are a believer in Jesus, then you are filled with the Holy Spirit, and when the Holy Spirit, the one who restrains evil, is taken out of the way, we who have the Holy Spirit dwelling within us will be taken with him. This is the rapture.

The Antichrist could be revealed when he signs the seven year covenant with Israel, but maybe not.
Daniel 9:27 states that he (the Antichrist) will confirm a covenant with many. The "many" could refer to many nations, but some seem to think it refers to the "many" people of Israel. It would seem, if "he" alone signs with Israel, then he would be revealed at that time, unless he had been revealed earlier. Or he could stay concealed if he signs the covenant with Israel along with *many* other nations. We should definitely know him for who he is when, after three and a half years, he breaks the terms of the covenant and he does away with the blood sacrifices. Certainly he will be known when he declares himself to be God. But whenever he is revealed, the rapture will have already happened.

Here are several scriptures which I believe give us the assurance that we who are believers in Jesus Christ, will not be on earth to experience this great tribulation.

(1.) Paul writes: "For God did not appoint us to suffer wrath but to receive salvation through our Lord Jesus Christ" (1 Thessalonians 5:9). To validate this verse as having reference to escaping the tribulation, the Bible Knowledge Commentary, which is an exposition of the scriptures by the Dallas Seminary Faculty states: "God's intention for them is not the **wrath** that will come on the earth in the day of the Lord, but the full salvation that will be theirs when the Lord returns for them in the clouds. The wrath of God referred to here clearly refers to the Tribulation; the context makes this apparent. Deliverance from that wrath is God's appointment for believers. This temporal salvation comes through the **Lord Jesus Christ** just as does eternal salvation." [1]

(2.) "They tell how you turned to God from idols to serve the living and true God, and to wait for his Son from heaven, whom he raised from the dead — Jesus, who rescues us from the coming wrath" (1 Thess. 1:9, 10). The wording is clear that God saves us from the wrath, not that he keeps us safe through it.

(3.) "Since you have kept my command to endure patiently, I will also keep you from the hour of trial that is going to come upon the whole world to test the inhabitants of the earth." (Revelation 3:10) It is clear from this passage that God will keep us from the trial, not take us through it, and not to extract us from the midst of it.

(4.) "Be careful, or your hearts will be weighed down with carousing, drunkenness and the anxieties of life, and that day will close on you suddenly like a trap. For it will come upon all those who live on the face of the whole earth. Be always on the watch, and pray that you may be able to escape all that is about to happen, and that you may be able to stand before the Son of Man." (Luke 21:34-36) Once again we see this day will come on all who live on the whole earth. But we who believe in Jesus will not be here to experience it.

(5.) "At that time Michael, the great prince who protects your people, will arise. There will be a time of distress such as has not happened from the beginning of nations until then. But at that time your people – everyone whose name is found written in the book – will be delivered." (Daniel 12:1) The way to get your name written in the book of life, is to believe in Jesus.

The following scripture does not speak of the rapture or the tribulation, but instead it shows the nature of our God, who in times of catastrophe, shows his willingness to select out of it, those he loves to spare them from the coming disaster. "For if God did not spare angels when they sinned, but sent them to hell, putting them chains of darkness to be held for judgment; if he did not spare the ancient world when he brought the flood on its ungodly people, but protected Noah, a preacher of righteousness, and seven others; if he condemned the cities of Sodom and Gomorrah by burning them to ashes, and made them an example of what is going to happen to the ungodly; and if he rescued Lot, a righteous man, who was distressed by the depraved conduct of the lawless (for that righteous man, living among them day after day, was tormented in his righteous soul by the lawless deeds he saw and heard) — if this is so, then the Lord knows how to rescue the godly from trials and to hold the unrighteous for punishment on the day of judgment. This is especially true of those who follow the corrupt desire of the flesh and despise authority." (2 Peter 2:4-10)

Another example of God's willingness to save his chosen from death is reported in Exodus chapters 11 and 12. Moses informs the Israelites that the Lord will bring one last plague on Egypt. The firstborn son of every family, including the firstborn of all livestock will die. To save their firstborn, the Israelites were instructed to place the blood of a lamb, in a specified way, on the top and sides of the door frames of their houses. That night, all the firstborn of all Egypt died, but all the firstborn of the Israelites lived. Because of the blood of the lamb, they were passed over.

Earlier in this chapter when I mentioned that you do not need to be concerned about what you are wearing at the time of the rapture, because we will all be changed in a twinkling of an eye, and changed from mortal to immortal, still there is, in a spiritual sense, a need to be appropriately dressed. In Matthew chapter 22, there is a parable that depicts a king who was holding a wedding feast for his son.

75

The people he had invited, had no interest, and each one, for his own reason, declined to attend. In his anger, the king dealt with those who would not attend. Then the king told his servants to invite anyone they could find to the banquet. Then when the king entered the banquet hall, he noticed one there who was not wearing wedding clothes. "He asked, 'how did you get in here without wedding clothes, friend?' The man was speechless. Then the king told the attendants, 'Tie him hand and foot, and throw him outside, into the darkness, where there will be weeping and gnashing of teeth'" (Matthew 22:12, 13).

Several times in Matthew and in Luke, there is a reference to the place of weeping and gnashing of teeth, and it is a reference to being cast into hell. It would seem unreasonable to cast the man into hell, just because he had on the wrong clothes, but there is a passage in Zechariah that might explain it. "Then he showed me Joshua the high priest standing before the angel of the Lord, and Satan standing at his right side to accuse him. The Lord said to Satan, 'The Lord rebuke you, Satan! The Lord, who has chosen Jerusalem, rebuke you! Is not this man a burning stick snatched from the fire?' Now Joshua was dressed in filthy clothes as he stood before the angel. The angel said to those who were standing before him, 'Take off his filthy clothes.' Then he said to Joshua, 'See, I have taken away your sin, and I will put fine garments on you'"
(Zechariah 3:1-4). In this scripture the filthy clothing of Joshua was symbolic of his sin. If this banquet represents acceptance of people for the rapture, then we must all be

wearing the clothing of perfect righteousness that can only be received by the grace of God, through faith in Jesus Christ. Through faith in Jesus Christ, our filthy clothing (sin) is taken away and we are clothed with the righteousness of Christ. This would explain why the wedding guest was cast into hell. He was not a believer in Jesus Christ; he was still dressed in his sin.

"I delight greatly in the Lord; my soul rejoices in my God. For he has clothed me with garments of salvation and arrayed me in a robe of his righteousness, as a bridegroom adorns his head like a priest, and as a bride adorns herself with her jewels." (Isaiah 61:10)

The rapture could occur at any moment. Make sure that you are ready by affirming your faith in Jesus Christ. When the taking away of all Christian believers from the earth, to meet with the Lord in the sky occurs, please be one of us. After the rapture, the horrible tribulation will be brought upon all those people who have been left behind.

Don't be left behind. Vaya con Dios! Go with God!

Swiftly and Suddenly Taken Away

"But God said to him, 'You fool! This very night your life will be demanded from you" Luke 12:20.

In vane rage the heathen murmur
"Let us break their bands asunder."
No one tells me what to do,
I'll be free from God and you.

No one knows the day or hour,
When the Lord will come with Power,
First the dead in Christ will rise,
Then His living to the skies.

Leading ladies locked in limbo,
Looks askance and arms akimbo,
Looking for some recognition,
Sinful souls that need redemption.

Many millionaires and many
Poor, but arrogant as any.
Empty vessel, empty heart,
In the Bridegroom, have no part.

Sheep to one side, goats the other.
Here the father, there the mother.
Sister and brother, are assigned,
Taken away, or left behind

Come to Jesus, all who hunger,
Come before your soul is plunder.
Don't have doubt or hesitation,
Today is *the* day of Salvation.

Chapter 6

The Security of the Believer

"For I am convinced that neither death nor life, neither angels nor demons, neither the present nor the future, nor any powers, neither height nor depth, nor anything else in all creation will be able to separate us from the love of God that is in Christ Jesus our Lord" (Romans 8:38, 39). This is our absolute and unshakeable guarantee of security.

We as believers in Jesus Christ can know that we believe, and are secure in our savior. We also know that we are not perfect. We still make mistakes, and sin. "If we claim to be without sin, we deceive ourselves and the truth is not in us" (1 John 1:8). Sin is not the problem for believers. As soon as John tells his fellow disciples that all of us have some sin in our lives, he immediately gives the perfect solution in the very next verse. "If we confess our sins, he is faithful and just and will forgive us our sins and purify us from all unrighteousness" (1 John 1:9). John had pointed out the obvious, that even though we believe in Jesus, even though we love him, we are not perfect, and we sin. But John also points out that through faith in Christ, confession to God with request to be forgiven brings righteousness. Therefore sin is not the real problem for Christians. The real problem, if a problem exists, is unbelief. When Christians, who by their faith, are in Christ, they have the certainty of eternal life. When Christians do not remain in Christ, their problem is unbelief. People who were in Christ, but chose to leave, either by specific unbelief, or just through disinterest in the Lord, which can be replaced by idolatry. That is the love of the things of this world, and personal pleasures. Jesus stresses this very point. "I am the vine; you are the branches. If you remain in me and I in you, you will bear much fruit; apart from me you can do nothing. If you do not remain in me, you are like a branch that is thrown away and withers; such branches are picked up, thrown into the fire and burned" (John 15:5, 6). Jesus is clearly saying that if a person is "in him", a true believer who by his faith is in Christ, and has the secure position of being "in him", and Jesus is in the believer, (The presence of the Holy Spirit), that believer will do many good works. Without Jesus, the good works cannot be done. He continues by explaining that if a believer who had the secure position of being in Christ, decides to leave that secure position, that one-time believer will suffer the same fate as the unbeliever. They will be thrown into the fire and burned.

This explanation by Jesus should be a sincere warning to individuals, or families who have wayward sons, daughters, or grandchildren, who at one time in their life accepted Jesus as their savior. Maybe they were also baptized, and read the Bible, and for a while seemed to be living for Christ. These children, even if they are now grown, if they have chosen to leave their dedication to the Lord, and for their own reasons, have left the church, and are living a life style that is worldly rather than righteous, they need to be ask about their faith in Jesus. Do not pat them on the back and say God loves you, if they have fallen away from their secure position in Christ. Tell them plainly there are things in their lives that God does not like, and they need to examine their lives in light of the Bible's teachings, repent of their sins, and rededicate their lives to Christ.

One of the examples of the "falling away" of a believer is given by Jesus when he explains the parable of the sower. "The seed falling on rocky ground refers to someone who hears the word and at once receives it with joy. But since they have no root, they last only a short time. When trouble or persecution comes because of the word, they quickly fall away" (Matthew 13:20, 21). The reference Jesus is making here, is a person who hears the gospel, the good news of eternal life through belief and obedience to Jesus Christ, they understand it, they believe it, and accept it in faith for themselves. But in time, they find they have opposition. Other acquaintances of theirs might laugh at them, or worse. This is possible for new believers of any age, but the very young might be the more vulnerable. Family and Christian friends should be very supportive of new believers. We should be encouraging them in their faith. The possibility of falling away from

Christ is always available for believers, and we are to be ever faithful, and constantly be renewing our faith.

"Therefore, dear friends, since you have been forewarned, be on your guard so that you may not be carried away by the error of lawless men and fall from your secure position" (2 Peter 3:17).

Jacob Arminius taught that a Christian could lose their salvation by leaving Christ, which is a loss of the promise of heaven, the salvation brought through faith.

John Calvin is known for his statement "A Christian can never lose their salvation". However, most Christians do not seem to know what he meant by that statement. If a Christian (meaning someone who has made a confession of Jesus as their savior, has been baptized, and lived a life honoring the Lord), ever leaves Jesus, for a life of godlessness, John Calvin says that person is lost, unsaved, and headed for the fires of Hell. John Calvin stresses that such a person does not lose their salvation, but that they never had salvation. To be true Christian, John Calvin insists that the person must persevere and be faithful to Jesus Christ until the end. If they ever fall away, then they never were a true Christian. So actually, John Calvin, and Jacob Arminius are in agreement about the terrible end of a person that we would call a Christian, if they should ever leave Christ.

We cannot know for sure, about the security of someone else, because we cannot know the true faith of another person. We sometimes believe that a person's faith is genuine because we love them and want them to be saved. But only God knows the heart. How many times have Christians, even pastors, priests, Bishops, or other Christians of high standing and recognition, been exposed as being some of the worst offenders? We don't know. God knows.

It is obvious in scripture that believers in Christ can, and do fall away from him, and from their faith. "The Spirit clearly says that in later times some will abandon the faith and follow deceiving spirits and things taught by demons" (1 Timothy 4:1). This is a scripture stating that believers in Christ, can and will abandon their faith, and believe lies.

"If they have escaped the corruption of the world by knowing our Lord and Savior Jesus Christ and are again entangled in it and overcome, they are worse off at the end than they were at the beginning. It would have been better for them not to have known the way of righteousness than to have known it and then to turn their backs on the sacred command that was passed on to them" (2 Peter 2:21).

In this verse, Peter is in agreement with Jacob Arminius, who believed that a Christian could lose their salvation, and in agreement with John Calvin who taught that if a person was not faithful to the end, they were lost.

There seem to be several ideas that Christian's have, that are not truly Biblical. One of the ideas that I have repeatedly heard is that a Christian goes immediately to heaven when they die. Support for this idea is a reference to Paul's comments in 2 Corinthians 5:6-8. The words commonly used are: "To be absent from the body, is to be present with the Lord." None of the Bibles I use have that exact wording, but even if Paul said those exact words, those words do not explain the concept that when a Christian dies, they go immediately to heaven. Paul would not have said that, because Paul did not believe that. In 1 Corinthians 15, Paul explains that when a Christian dies, they sleep in the grave, awaiting the first resurrection, which is the rapture. "So will it be with the resurrection of the dead. The body that is sown is perishable, it is raised imperishable" (1Corinthians 15:42). Paul continues: "Listen, I tell you a mystery: We will not all sleep, but we will all be changed – in a flash, in the twinkling of an eye, at the last trumpet. For the trumpet will sound, the dead will be raised imperishable, and we will be changed. For the perishable must clothe itself with the imperishable, and the mortal with immortality, then the saying that is written will come true: "Death has been swallowed up in victory" (1Corinthians 15:51, 54). In these verses, Paul gives another reason that Christians do not go to heaven when they die. In verse 50 he said "flesh and blood cannot inherit the kingdom of God, nor does the perishable inherit the imperishable." We won't go to heaven until we are immortal.

We are not now immortal. We do not become immortal until the rapture, which is the first resurrection. Since at the rapture, the dead in Christ rise first, it is because they have been sleeping in the grave.

People sometimes refer to their "spirit". If they are referring to the "life" that the Lord God has breathed into them, then that is an acceptable term. It would be a mistake to think that we have a body, a soul, and a spirit. We don't have all three. We, like Adam, have only two parts. "Then the Lord God formed a man from the dust of the ground and breathed into his nostrils the breath of life, and the man became a living being" (Genesis 2:7). Some versions of the Bible say "a living soul". Either way, Adam had only two parts, he had a physical body made of the chemical compounds that are indigenous to the earth, and he had life, that was God breathed into his nostrils. This is the one thing that modern science cannot do. They cannot give life. We are the same as Adam, we only have two parts, a physical body, and life. That life can be referred to as our soul, or as our spirit. We sometimes speak of a person's spirit, meaning their attitude. They might have the spirit of adventure.

"For the word of God is alive and active. Sharper than any double-edged sword, it penetrates even to dividing soul and spirit, joints and marrow; it judges the thoughts and attitudes of the heart" (Hebrews 4:12). Since we only have two parts, body and soul, this scripture must be

85

speaking of a person's soul, being separated from the Holy Spirit of God. Some believe that could never happen, but I believe it does happen when a believer in Christ, leaves Christ as Jesus explains in John 15:5, 6. Also this, "Now the Spirit of the Lord had departed from Saul, and an evil spirit from the Lord tormented him" (1 Samuel 16:14). "My love will never be taken away as I took it from Saul" (2 Samuel 7:15).

It seems that many Christians believe that as soon as we believe in Jesus Christ, and receive the Holy Spirit, that we receive eternal life at that time. However, Paul makes it clear that we do not receive eternal life until the rapture, which is the first resurrection, 1 Corinthians 15:50-58.

Many times throughout the Bible, the term sleep has been used for death. "Multitudes who sleep in the dust of the earth will awake: some to everlasting life, others to shame and everlasting contempt" (Daniel 12:2). And also this: "Do not be amazed at this, for a time is coming when all who are in their graves will hear his voice and come out – those who have done what is good will rise to live, and those who have done what is evil will rise to be condemned" (John 5:28, 29) The term "sleep" is used again when Jesus referred to the death of Lazarus: "After he had said all this, he went on to tell them, 'Our friend Lazarus has fallen asleep; but I am going there to wake him up.'

His disciples replied, 'Lord, if he sleeps, he will get better.' Jesus had been speaking of his death, but his disciples thought he meant natural sleep.

So then he told them plainly, 'Lazarus is dead, and for your sake I am glad I was not there, so that you may believe. But let us go to him" (John 11:11-15).

Let me ask a question that I don't know the answer to. Is Charles Templeton saved? In the late 1940s, two evangelists left for Europe to start a great Christian crusade. The leader of the two was Charles Templeton, the second man was Billy Graham. Shortly after they started preaching, Charles Templeton left, explaining that he had lost his faith in God. Some years later, he wrote the book *Farewell to God: My Reasons for Rejecting the Christian Faith.* Where is he now? I'm sure I don't know, it is not for me to say, but my opinion is that his faith in God was genuine. For years he had been a faithful Christian, whose faithful service placed him in this elevated position of being a world evangelist. He was a brilliant graduate of Princeton University who had amazing debating skills because of his impressive knowledge of the Bible. Over time, he found that he could not accept the idea of an almighty and loving God who would allow the existence of an eternal Hell, he doubted the Genesis account of creation. By the time he wrote his book, he had experienced a serious decline of his mental faculties. His later decision to say farewell to God, was a choice that each of us have the freedom to make for ourselves. It is the grace of God that assures us of our eternal security through our continuing faith in Jesus Christ. Where is Charles Templeton today? It is sufficient for us that our Almighty God knows.

There is a misunderstanding of true and living faith in the Lord, which could be disastrous. It has to do with many people who consider themselves to be Christian, or with our loved ones whom we believe to be secure. I must tread most cautiously here. For I am not the one who decides your eternal destination. That is the Lord's domain. I am not usurping his authority here, but only sounding a caution. Consider my own life. Raised in a home where Sunday church was as regular as the calendar, I received Jesus as my savior at age eleven, I was baptized and joined the church. At age thirteen I had second thoughts and started leaving the church in my mind, and at seventeen, I physically left the church for the next twenty-five years. Even in that twenty-fifth year, had anyone asked me, "Are you a Christian?" I'm sure I would have answered yes. Even though I had never read more than two or three pages of the Bible in my lifetime and did not own a Bible. Even though I had not been a church attendee in twenty-five years, I did not pray, I used his name somewhat frequently but not in a respectful way. But I remembered in my youth, I had believed in Christ and had been baptized, so I probably would have said, yes, I am a Christian. I fear there are many in the world today somewhat like that, even though, every case is individually different.

Starting in 1975, I had four dreams. Although I dream a great deal, these four dreams have always been special, and they have always been connected for me. They happened several months apart, probably over the period of a year or so. This is a brief outline of those four dreams. The first was one of peace, and the thought that God loved me, and that no harm would come to me. The second dream was one of some anxiety, since I was high in the air, at the very bottom of a wooden scaffold structure, being supported only by the lateral pressure I could exert against two vertical beams, one in front of me, the other behind me. Below me was nothing, forever. It was an uncomfortable position. In the third dream, I was in a mountain valley, very cool and after sunset but still with some faint light in the sky, enough to see the outlines of the mountains. I was looking up at a large, old style railroad trestle. Then I saw the train, coming from my right, crossing the trestle, then turning west and going away from me. I could see the people in the dining car, eating and talking and the warm golden light streaming out of the windows. I wanted to be on that train. I wanted to be with those nice people. I knew they were going to heaven, and I could not go with them. Then I noticed there was a chain link fence projecting from the rail bed, keeping me out. On top of that fencing was barbed wire. It was hopeless. Then I noticed that one of the sections of fence was missing. There was a way! I won't spend much time with my fourth dream, but I was in Satan's house. It seemed like a lazy Saturday morning, and I was in the game room, waiting for a pool game, which was how I had been spending most of my free time when awake. Realizing that it was Satan's house and feeling uncomfortable and wanting to leave, I pulled the eight-inch steel file from my hip pocket, which had been my defensive weapon when I had been playing pool in many unsavory places, when a young boy of Satan's household looked down at the file and smirked, "What good do you think that will do you?" My spirit sank.

Those four dreams are with me today, but they did not change my life at that time. Some time, months later on, my sister told me she had just bought a Bible that was in plain English and easy to understand. I had always thought the King James Version was too old-style in its language to be understood. I don't feel that way today. Then, a few weeks later, a radio station I had been listening to in my car, had stopped playing Classical music, and had gone to a gospel program where they were talking about Job. Possibly the oldest book in the Bible. About 3000 years old. And Job said that God has spread out the north over empty space, and hung the earth on nothing. That irritated me. I changed the station. But for days and weeks, I could not get that idea out of my head. It was my opinion that early civilizations did not know this. I thought they believed the earth was held up by an elephant, or by Atlas, or Roman pillars or something. For some reason, I felt offended that they would say something about the Bible that was not true. They had done it to me. They had planted a seed that would not stop growing. I had to know. Then, remembering my sister's comment about a Bible in plain English, called the *Living Bible*, I went to the store and bought one. Being a very poor reader, I could not find it by scanning through. I decided that no matter how long it took, I was going to start reading the book of Job at chapter 1 and verse 1, and read it word by word, until I would either find it, or know that they were lying. Wouldn't you know it? Chapter 26 verse 7: "God stretches out heaven over empty space and hangs the earth on nothing" (TLB). Well, imagine my surprise. I read the rest of the book of Job, then set the Bible down for a few more months. But at least, I now owned a Bible.

Some time later, I recalled that a friend in high school had told me that no one could understand the book of Revelation. This was because it was so mystical. The thought occurred to me, now I have a Bible in plain English. I think I'll read it, since it would obviously be understandable, in plain English. I read about half of it, then set the Bible down. It wasn't what I expected, and I did not want to read any more of it. I went to bed.

The next night, brave or not, I had to know what the rest of it said. Astounding. It was awesome. It was frightening. It was convicting. I was in the midst of an eternal battle, God was going to win, and I was on the wrong side.

For the first time in 25 years, I knelt on the floor to pray. "Now I lay me down to sleep. . ." That was all I knew. When I finished, I said Lord, that's not going to cut it. We need to talk. I poured out my soul, my sin, my failures, to the depth of my heart. That started my prayer life, and started the practice of reading the Bible for hours every morning and every evening without fail. I started going to many different churches, listening to Christian radio, and watching Christian TV. It was a change of life.

But now back to the reason I told you all this. Had I lost my salvation? Was I on the verge of losing my salvation? Many will say I had not lost it. I believe that the Lord gave me those four dreams, and the radio aggravation about Job, and my sister's information about a new Bible, and the curiosity about Revelation, all for the purpose of calling me back from my bad choices, which may have eternally separated me from the love of God. Since I don't know the absolute answer on this subject, I will just give you my opinion. Don't preach "once saved, always saved" because it might give confidence to the apostate. Apostasy is when a believer in Jesus Christ, willfully and continually denies their faith in Christ. It might give confidence to some who might have the opinion, I prayed the prayer when I was young, and therefore I am eternally secure. Or I was baptized, or christened, or confirmed, or I think I believed when I was younger, or, I know about God, therefore I'm sure he loves me. This could be the loss of everything. Salvation is not through some superficial action taken because of the coercion of others, but through living faith in Jesus Christ. Obeying is believing, disobeying is unbelief. But if salvation is by the grace of God to all who believe in Jesus, what happens if a person loses their faith. Do they also lose their salvation? Can faith in Jesus be lost? Is that possible? I believe is possible by drifting away, and I give my own life as an example. I believe I was at the cross-roads and God in his mercy was getting my attention, and calling me back. I don't know, but I don't want to risk it, and I don't think you should risk it either. Why preach security to those who may need a calling back to the righteousness of faith? The doctrine of the security of the believer is absolutely true, and irrefutable, for believers. But the ultra-nice so-called doctrine of "once saved, always saved' has probably been responsible for more people ending up in Hell, than any other saying, or practice of the church. It has caused parents, grandparents, and others to not approach their loved ones to implore them to return to God. To return to loving and obeying Jesus Christ, and repenting of their sins and failures, so they might be saved. This teaching gives confidence to the apostate, and causes their loved ones to say: "Well, they are not living for Christ today, that's for sure, but I know I will see them in heaven because they were baptized when they were eleven." If they have left Christ, then I don't think you will see them in heaven. How many souls, who have drifted away from Christ, could have been saved by loving advice to return to Jesus in repentance and obedience?

When Satan was created, he was a powerful servant of God. When he rebelled against God, he was cast out of heaven, and the lake of fire was created for him. If Satan, who truly knew God, can choose to leave God, then I suspect we can make the same choice. Still, always remember. We do not decide who is righteous in their faith, God does. Whew! That's a relief.

Thinking of Satan brings to mind a misconception which all of us have heard repeatedly. Power corrupts, and absolute power corrupts absolutely. Humbug! This is a false statement. It is like another frequent misquotation of the Bible: Money is the root of all evil. Again humbug. The Bible states in 1 Timothy 6:10 "For the love of money is a root of all kinds of evil." It isn't money that causes the problem. It is the love of money that can lead to all kinds of evil. Lusting for money can lead to many kinds of sin. Money by itself in not a problem, it is only a tool which we can use for good or evil. It is the same way with power. Power is a tool which can be used for good, or for evil. It is not power that corrupts. It is the love of power which can corrupt. Power used for good honors God. And as far as absolute power is concerned, there is only one who possesses absolute power and that is the Lord God Almighty, and in him there is no corruption. However, there is only one I know of who lusts for absolute power, and that is Satan, and in him is absolute corruption. Now at least we have that settled.

The doctrine of the security of the believer has never saved anyone. It is not a doctrine of salvation. What it has done, when it has been expanded to be "once saved, always saved" has given confidence to those who are in need of repentance. We do not have the ability to know when someone else is saved. We only have the outside evidence. Only God knows the heart, and it is God who decides their disposition.

Chapter 7

Eternal Punishment?

Will the "unsaved" be in torment forever? God, in the Bible, explains why they will *not* be in torment forever.

Only those who are immortal will live forever.

We are mortal. We are not immortal. We are perishable.

"Then the Lord said, "My Spirit will not contend with humans forever, for they are mortal; their days will be a hundred and twenty years" (Genesis 6:3). A hundred and twenty years is a limited time of mortality.

"For God so loved the world that he gave his one and only Son, that whoever believes in him shall not perish but have eternal life" (John 3:16). The Lord is telling us we have two choices. Either we believe in Jesus and have eternal life, or we do not believe in him, and perish. The word perish means to cease to exist. We are perishable! This same idea is repeated in John 3:36 "Whoever believes in the Son has eternal life, but whoever rejects the Son will not see life". Life eternal is given to those who believe in

Jesus, but eternal life is not given to those who do not believe in him.

"And the Lord God formed man of the dust of the ground, and breathed into his nostrils the breath of life; and man became a living soul" (Genesis 2:7 KJV). Adam was created body and soul. Neither body nor soul are eternal, they are mortal. Mortal means perishable. Body and soul can cease to exist. Adam's soul was the life that the Lord God had breathed into his nostrils. Body and soul are both perishable, not imperishable. "Do not be afraid of those who kill the body but cannot kill the soul. Rather, be afraid of the One who can destroy both soul and body in hell" (Matthew 10:28). Both body and soul can be destroyed. They are not immortal.

"For the wages of sin is death" (Romans 6:23). The wages of sin is death, not eternal punishment.

"—they will be consigned to the fiery lake of burning sulfur. This is the second death" (Revelation 21:8). The lake of fire will be the second death. Our first death is when our body dies. In the Bible, this first death is referred to as "sleep". The second death is after the second resurrection, for all whose names are not written in the book of life. Because their names are not written in the book of life, they have not received immortality, they are still mortal, meaning that they are still perishable. The lake of fire was created for the devil and his angels (See Matthew 25:41) and it is an eternal fire. The devil and his angles will be in torment in this eternal fire, forever. The mortal people who are cast in there, will perish.

"Did God really say, 'You must not eat from any tree in the garden'". "The woman said to the serpent, 'We may eat fruit from the trees in the garden, but God did say, "You must not eat fruit from the tree that is in the middle of the garden, and you must not touch it, or you will die." "You will not certainly die," the serpent said to the woman" (Genesis 3:1-4).

There were two trees in the middle of the garden, the tree of life, and the tree of the knowledge of good and evil. (See: Genesis 2:9). Eve and Adam ate from the tree of the knowledge of good and evil.

"When the woman saw that the fruit of the tree was good for food and pleasing to the eye, and also desirable for gaining wisdom, she took some and ate it. She also gave some to her husband, who was with her, and he ate it" (Genesis 3:6).

"And the Lord God said, 'The man has now become like one of us, knowing good and evil. He must not be allowed to reach out his hand and take also from the tree of life and eat, and live forever'" (Genesis 3:22). When Adam and Eve sinned against God, they were expelled them from the garden, and God made sure that they would not be able to get back in, and eat fruit from the tree of life and live forever and become immortal. "So the Lord God banished him from the Garden of Eden to work the ground from which he had been taken. After he drove the man out, he placed on the east side of the Garden of Eden cherubim and a flaming sword flashing back and forth to guard the way to the tree of life" (Genesis 3:23, 24). God's plan for mankind was to give them the opportunity for eternal life, but only after Jesus Christ had made full payment for their sins, not now in the garden where they had just separated themselves from God by sin, when they broke God's law.

Speaking of Jesus, the apostle John wrote: "Yet to all who did receive him, to those who believed in his name, he gave the right to become children of God – children born not of natural descent, nor of human decision or a husband's will, but born of God" (John 1:12). To all who believe in him (Jesus), God has given the right to become children of God. God has not made them children of God, but has given them the right to "become" children of God. At the time of our believing in Christ Jesus, we do not become immortal, but we have the right to become immortal. Even those believers in Jesus, who have died, are not yet immortal. They await the time for their change into immortality, as do we the living believers, and that time will be at the rapture.

"So will it be with the resurrection of the dead. The body that is sown is perishable, it is raised imperishable;" (1 Corinthians 15:42).

"I declare to you, brothers and sisters, that flesh and blood cannot inherit the kingdom of God, nor does the perishable inherit the imperishable. Listen, I tell you a mystery: We will not all sleep, but we will all be changed – in a flash, in the twinkling of an eye, at the last trumpet. For the trumpet will sound, the dead will be raised imperishable, and we will be changed. For the perishable must clothe itself with the imperishable, and the mortal with immortality. When the perishable has been clothed with the imperishable, and the mortal with immortality, then the saying that is written will come true: "Death has been swallowed up in victory."

"Where, O death, is your victory?

Where, O death, is your sting?"
1 Corinthians 15:50-55).

The people who are saved through faith in Jesus, will receive their immortality at the rapture, which is the first resurrection. The people who are unsaved will not be given immortality. They are still perishable. So when the perishable unsaved people are cast into the lake of fire, they will perish. They will cease to exist.

Just because the "unsaved" will not be in torment forever, because they are mortal and will perish, that does not give them any reason to rejoice. There is promised a time of punishment in Hell for those who do not receive forgiveness of their sins through faith in Jesus Christ. Hell is a very real place of torment and is referred to by Jesus many times. Sometimes called Hell, sometimes Hades, or Gehenna. In Matthew and Luke there are several scriptures that refer to the outer darkness, or the fiery furnace where there is weeping and gnashing of teeth. These are also references to Hell. This is a very real place of torment for the unsaved. The story of the rich man and Lazarus is considered to be a reference to actual people, because Lazarus called by his name, and in parables, personal names are not used. This is a story, told by Jesus, that tells of a rich man who suffered in the agony of Hell.

"There was a rich man who was dressed in purple and fine linen and lived in luxury every day. At his gate was laid a beggar named Lazarus, covered with sores and longing to eat what fell from the rich man's table. Even the dogs came and licked his sores.

The time came when the beggar died and the angels carried him to Abraham's side. The rich man also died and was buried. In Hades, where he was in torment, he looked up and saw Abraham far away, with Lazarus by his side. So he called to him, 'Father Abraham, have pity on me and send Lazarus to dip the tip of his finger in water and cool my tongue, because I am in agony in this fire.'

"But Abraham replied, 'Son, remember that in your lifetime you received your good things, while Lazarus received bad things, but now he is comforted here and you are in agony. And besides all this, between us and you a great chasm has been set in place, so that those who want to go from here to you cannot, nor can anyone cross over from there to us'" (Luke 16:26).

This tale sounds to be in the past tense. It is told to as something that has already happened. I still have difficulty in accepting that Idea because that would mean that the rich man was cast into Hell before he had his judgment. The unsaved are not judged until after the second resurrection, so how is it just to cast him into Hell, without his "day in court". How else could his proper sentence be assessed? Of course it can be done by God.

Well, whatever the answer is, Hell is real and to be avoided at any and all costs. Faith in Christ is free of cost for you, because Jesus has already paid the cost, in full.

When will things that are perishable, cease to exist? According to the laws given in the Old Testament, the appropriate punishments varied to suit the crime. If unbelievers in Christ Jesus are cast into Hell, how long must they suffer there, before they perish? We don't know. This is Gods decision, and he is just and fair. When Death and Hell are thrown into the lake of fire, that will certainly cause to "perish" everything that is perishable, and not eternal. But death and Hell are not cast into the lake of fire until after the millennium, which is the one thousand year reign of Christ. And the millennium will not start until after the rapture and the seven year tribulation.

"And I saw an angel coming down out of heaven, having the key to the Abyss and holding in his hand a great chain. He seized the dragon, that ancient serpent, who is the devil, or Satan, and bound him for a thousand years. He threw him into the Abyss, and locked and sealed it over him, to keep him from deceiving the nations anymore until the thousand years were ended. After that, he must be set free for a short time" (Revelation 20:1-3). "The sea gave up the dead that were in it, and death and Hades gave up the dead that were in them, and each person was judged according to what they had done. Then death and Hades were thrown into the lake of fire. The lake of fire is the second death. Anyone whose name was not found written in the book of life was thrown into the lake of fire" (Revelation 20:13-15). So, even though these unsaved persons will ultimately perish, their time of punishment in Hell could be extremely long. I believe that everything the Lord God does is right. Whatever he does will be appropriate. He is not unjust, quite the contrary, he is the only one who is just. All sentences and punishments will be exactly what is deserved. No more, and no less. The only thing that might seem unreasonable is the grace of God which we can receive through faith in Jesus Christ.

People cast into Hell will not be punished equally. The Bible does not say this, but the examples in the Bible of punishments that God decrees for breaking the laws, are as many and varied as the laws that are broken. Minor offences receive minor punishment, while more serious offences receive a more serious penalty. For example:

"The servant who knows the master's will and does not get ready or does not do what the master wants will be beaten with many blows. But the one who does not know and does things deserving punishment will be beaten with few blows" (Luke 12:47, 48).

There is only one scripture I know of in the entire Bible that indicates, some humans will suffer in the lake of fire, forever. "A third angel followed them and said in a loud voice: 'If anyone worships the beast and its image and receives its mark on their forehead or on their hand, they, too, will drink the wine of God's fury, which has been poured full strength into the cup of his wrath. They will be tormented with burning sulfur in the presence of the holy angels and of the Lamb. And the smoke of their torment will rise forever and ever. There will be no rest day or night for those who worship the beast and its image, or for anyone who receives the mark of its name.' This calls for patient endurance on the part of the people of God who keep his commands and remain faithful to Jesus" (Revelation 14:9-12). This verse does not apply to anyone who has lived from the time of Adam and Eve until now, it *only* applies to those people who are alive on earth, at the time of the rule of the Antichrist, and who worship the beast and/or its image, or who receive the mark of its name. The reason that these people will suffer eternally is not given, but I suspect that in worshiping the beast and/or its image, or by taking the mark of its name, they will so completely identify themselves with Satan, that they will be "in him" forever. It will be infinitely better for anyone

103

living at that time, to refuse to worship the beast or take its mark, and instead to have faith in Jesus Christ and call on him to save you, which no doubt will cause you to be killed, but because you now express your faith in Jesus Christ, you will receive eternal life in heaven. You will certainly not be alone in doing this. In Revelation chapter 7, it refers to a multitude that no one could count, people from every tribe, people, nation and language, who had come out of the great tribulation because they had called on Jesus. "They have washed their robes and made them white in the blood of the Lamb" (Revelation 7:14). They too have received eternal life in heaven because they did not worship the beast and its image, or taken the mark of its name, but have instead called on the name of the Lord Jesus Christ!

Even if the people cast into Hell suffer for their sin, and then ultimately perish, that is not the horror of going to Hell. The dreadful part is, they will not spend eternity in heaven with the Lord our God.

Don't be one of those who is cast into the lake of fire. It's time for you to become one of us. Praise God!

Chapter 8

Time

180

The quotidian meridian that changes the date,
From Sunday to Monday, to early from late,
Is in the Pacific, specifically placed,
From Bering, past Midway, so time's interlaced.

Time has been described as the distance between events. It is the duration of the event. Nothing can exist in the absence of time. Time is one of the inseparable identities of the universe, along with matter and space. Time is always positive, never negative. The arrow of time goes forward, never backward. Omar Khayyam who lived about the year eleven hundred, Anno Domini, realized this when in his *Rubaiyat* he wrote:

"The Moving Finger writes and, having writ,
Moves on: nor all thy Piety nor Wit
Shall lure it back to cancel half a line,
Nor all thy Tears wash out a Word of it." [1]

105

Time travel is not only possible, it is imperative. We cannot avoid it. We constantly travel forward through time, as Omar Khayyam noticed. That is not the problem.

Shall we travel backward into time and change the past, and so alter the present? Many stories have been written on this subject, and I must admit that I have been fascinated with them, from the H. G. Wells story *The Time Machine*, which was certainly not the first to deal with the subject, but may have been the first to be written well enough to have wide public interest, to the more modern ones like *Star Trek*, and others. The ideas presented are fascinating fiction in the purest sense, which allows us to travel vicariously on the mental wings of our imagination. However, let's get one thing clear. To travel backward in time is humanly impossible.

To start with one of the simplest perplexities, let's say you traveled backward into time for a distance of one year. Then you use a 45-caliber pistol to blow your brains out. Well then, it seems perfectly clear that you were not alive here today to do any time traveling, because you died a year ago.

Then I suppose there is the question, when you go back a year, and blow out your brains, do you place the gun to your head, as you would today, or do you place the gun to the head of your body, which existed a year ago, and is a year younger than you are now? In other words, if you go back to a place where you already are, do you say hello to yourself? How much insanity is necessary before you see that traveling backward in time is not humanly possible.

Still, another thought comes to mind. If you were to travel backward into time for one year, what would you see. Describe it to me. Do you remember where you were a year ago? Would you like to return there? Well then, let's examine your dilemma. The Earth is traveling around the Sun at the approximate speed of three times ten to the fourth meters per second, or about 67,000 miles per hour. And you may have thought that you had only traveled at maximum speed of about a few hundred or so miles an hour. (a few thousand miles per hour if you are a Blackbird pilot, or an astronaut.) But the big speed comes from the fact that our part of the Milky Way Galaxy is expanding at the rate of about 671,000 miles per hour, or about 5.88 billion miles per year. To put this number in perspective, the planet Pluto is about 3.67 billion miles from the Sun. Therefore, if you go backward in time, to the place you were one year ago, you will be in deep space, well beyond our Solar system. There is no Oxygen there, but not to worry. The temperature is something approaching absolute zero, that is about four hundred and fifty some degrees below zero on the Fahrenheit scale, but not to worry. Before you can be asphyxiated, or frozen to death, you will explode, because you will be in a nearly perfect vacuum. Do you really want to go back there? Why?

Perhaps you might think that your "time machine" will have the ability to replace things as they were in a previous time. A machine like that would be quite valuable, after all, the world is paying a high price for energy, and a machine that could generate that much energy would be in high demand, even if it could not go backward in time. I wonder exactly how much energy it would take to stop the Earth in its motion, and reverse its motion to its position in a previous time. It doesn't seem right to go back without taking the Sun too. In fact, you will probably need to stop the entire universe in its accelerated expansion, reverse it to its position in a previous time, and then comes the tricky part. It needs to be restarted on its original path, hopefully without anyone noticing the change. Certainly, people would notice if the coffee were jostled out of their cup. The sad news is, at that time, you and the universe would be at the age you were a year ago, plus the next year that had already transpired, plus the time it took to go back. Traveling backward in time is humanly impossible.

There are however, matters which are exceedingly beyond the mind and understanding of humans. "Jesus replied, "What is impossible with men is possible with God" (Luke 18:27).

"Isaiah answered, 'This is the Lord's sign to you that the Lord will do what he has promised: Shall the shadow go forward ten steps, or shall it go back ten steps?' 'It is a simple matter for the shadow to go forward ten steps,' said Hezekiah. 'Rather, have it go back ten steps.' Then the prophet Isaiah called upon the Lord, and the Lord made the shadow go back the ten steps it had gone down on the stairway of Ahaz." (2 Kings 20:9 -11)

"On the day the Lord gave the Amorites over to Israel, Joshua said to the Lord in the presence of Israel:

'Sun, stand still over Gibeon,
And you moon, over the Valley of Aijalon.'
So the sun stood still,
and the moon stopped,
till the nation avenged itself on its enemies,

as it is written in the Book of Jashar. The sun stopped in the middle of the sky and delayed going down about a full day. There has never been a day like it before or since, a day when the Lord listened to a human being. Surely the Lord was fighting for Israel!

Then Joshua returned with all Israel to the camp at Gilgal" (Joshua 10:12-15).

Why do I talk about ideas of time? Because time is mentioned repeatedly in the Bible, and it does not always mean the same thing. "But do not forget this one thing, dear friends: With the Lord a day is like a thousand years, and a thousand years are like a day. The Lord is not slow in keeping his promise, as some understand slowness. Instead he is patient with you, not wanting anyone to perish, but everyone to come to repentance" (2 Peter 3:8,9).

The time that we experience, and the time in which God exists, is different.

The first verse in the Bible speaks of time. "In the beginning God created the heavens and the earth" (Genesis 1:1). That was the beginning of time, as we know it. However, God has existed eternally. Don't ask me to explain eternity, which, it seems, always has been and always will be, I cannot fathom it. That is God's realm. But astrophysicists have told us that at creation, which some of them would rather refer to as "the big bang", there were ten dimensions. Only four of these were unwound so that we can experience them. They were the three dimensions of length, width, and height, the three physical dimensions, and the fourth dimension of time. It seems that time should be the first, because without a time for something to exist, there can be no physical matter to exist. I mention this because Genesis 1:1 refers to the beginning, which is the beginning of all things in existence. Still, all things were created by God who is eternal spirit, who must exist in a different sort of time, since what we call time only came into existence at creation, but God's time is separate from that, which is difficult to comprehend. Even though he has given us some glimpses of it, like the afore mentioned 2 Peter 3:8, 9. Chapter 1 of Genesis covers the first six days of the creation, what we casually refer to as the creation of "everything". Were these days each a twenty-four-hour period? Well, I don't know. They could have been, but the Sun, by which we measure days, was not created until the fourth day. I don't know, but I strongly suspect that these first "days" were great, long, periods of time. Sometimes, the term day is used for something different than a twenty-four-hour period. The day of the Lord refers to the seven years of tribulation. As a geologist, I took the word of others who claimed to know what they were talking about, when they claimed that the earth was billions of years old. It seemed to be reasonable at the time, and I still believe they have come to a reasonable conclusion. The important thing is, it doesn't matter. We don't have to know that. Christians, and some of other religions and other mind sets, refer to this period of time as the creation. Whenever it was, and however long it took, God did it. As far as the big bang is concerned, it seems more logical to think of the creation of everything from nothing, as being by the plan, power, and design of the absolute Almighty and eternal God, rather than to think that all things came into existence from nothing, by the power, plan, and design of nothing. It seems that if there ever were a time when there was absolutely nothing, and no God, then there never could be anything. Isn't that sound physics?

Here is another poser on time. Suppose that there actually were an almighty God. The eternally existing God of the Bible, in whom the Christians and Jews believe. This God would have all power and authority to do whatever he wanted to do, which is immeasurably beyond your knowledge or your imagination. Such a God would have it in his power to have created the entire universe we know, plus countless others, and he would have the power and ability to have created all of this, only five minutes ago. He would have the power and ability to have done this, and at that time to have given you and the rest of us, the memories we have which give us confidence that we have been alive for years. We can remember our childhood and what we did last week, but our memories were given to us only five minutes ago, when God brought all things into existence. To think that this might have actually happened is preposterous. The only reason I mention it is to show you, that your brilliant mind is only a finite human mind, it is incapable of proving that you were not created five minutes ago. You are only human while the Lord is eternally God.

In the book of Daniel, a period of seventy weeks is referred to in such a way that we conclude that the weeks are indeed periods of seven years, rather than seven days. A study of the prophecy in the book of Daniel reveals that all of the prophecies of the first sixty-nine of these "weeks" have already transpired, and we are now in that time gap between the sixty-ninth and the seventieth week. This seventieth week is the last time period of seven years wherein the final battle of Armageddon takes place, followed by the second coming of the Lord Jesus Christ.

There is another very important recognition of the value of time. You only have so much time in a day. How much of that time do you need for entertainment? Does the entertainment you chose make you feel satisfied? Does it draw you closer to God? Does it advance the kingdom of

God on earth? There are books about people, history, hobbies, Christian life and practice, and many books of interest that you could read, without being interrupted every few minutes with many long, loud commercials. You could spend your spare time improving your mind, instead of needing to be entertained by television programs of questionable value. There are ways that only you can decide on, which would better spend the very limited time you have. Do you have family? Are you getting and giving the valuable time of being family? It is not necessary to always plan events, or to plan this, that, or something special. Just being there is good. It is important. Time.

Directions to Heaven

Chapter 9

Is it bad to Hate?

Hate is not a crime; it is an opinion.

God hates sin.

When was the last time you heard a good sermon explaining to us how we should be good haters? Have you ever heard one? Why not? We are commanded by God to be good haters. Jesus was a good hater, and he received a special anointing because of it. We need to be good haters like Jesus.

God has always commanded us to hate. "Hate evil, love good;" (Amos 5:15). That is a message from God to his people. That should be easy. Love what is of God, and hate anything that tends to destroy what is good. Old Testament you say? Not for us today? Then why did Paul repeat it, "Love must be sincere. Hate what is evil; cling to what is good" (Romans 12:9). If hate is a bad thing, why does the Lord God, speaking about Jesus say: "You have loved righteousness and hated wickedness; therefore God, your God has set you above your companions by anointing you with the oil of joy" (Hebrews 1:9).

115

Jesus hated the cross, despising its shame. "fixing our eyes on Jesus, the pioneer and perfector of faith. For the joy set before him he endured the cross, scorning its shame, and sat down at the right hand of the throne of God" (Hebrews 12:2).

When Jesus entered the temple, and saw it being disgraced and dishonored by the tradesmen, it made him angry. "Jesus entered the temple courts and drove out all who were buying and selling there. He overturned the tables of the money changers and the benches of those selling doves. 'It is written,' he said to them, 'My house will be called a house of prayer, but you are making it a den of robbers'" (Matthew 21: 12, 13). He hated what they were doing, it made him angry, and it moved him to action, to drive out and rebuke the sinners.

If you have tolerance for evil, or if you ignore evil, you disobey God. He has repeatedly commanded you to hate evil. Do not think that you are being loving, you are not. It is probably closer to the truth that you are being cowardly. Even if you feel powerless in stopping it, you can pray, but you must hate all that God hates, and hate all that that violates his truth. There are times when even though we hate sin, we might find ourselves in a situation when speaking up to oppose it, could be dangerous. I don't mean that others might disagree with you. I mean they might very well attack you. At times like these, you must decide what, if anything, to say. Having reasonable discretion can be wise.

We should hate what God hates, and love what God loves, isn't that simple enough? What does God hate? Please do not just skim over these seven items. Read each one, and consider it. "There are six things the Lord hates, seven that are detestable to him:

haughty eyes,
a lying tongue,
hands that shed innocent blood,
a heart that devises wicked schemes,
feet that are quick to rush into evil,
a false witness who pours out lies
and a person who stirs up conflict in
the community" (Proverbs 6:16-19 NKJV).

Was that six or seven? Actually, there were seven entries but only six items, because lying was mentioned twice.

Do not think that God loves to hate. It is because of hateful sin, that God loved us enough to die for us, and offer us a way to be healed from our sin, and saved from the consequences of our sin. So, God hates the sin that separates us from him. Still, "he is patient with you, not wanting anyone to perish, but everyone to come to repentance" (2 Peter 3:9).

What else does God hate?

117

Examine the 10 commandments:

having other gods before him
idolatry
misusing his name
dishonoring your father or mother
murdering
committing adultery
stealing
lying – giving false testimony
coveting
See: Revelation 21:8
cowardly
unbelievers
vile
murders
sexual immoral
those who practice the magic arts
idolaters
and all liars

God hates sin. It is sin that took Jesus to the cross. Sin is breaking God's law. Sin is probably being anything less than the perfect righteousness of Jesus. Are you sinful? It is because we all have sinned and fall short of the glory of God, that we all need a savior.

When we obey and follow Jesus, we are hated by the world, but we are loved by God.

"If the world hates you, keep in mind that it hated me first. If you belonged to the world, it would love you as its own. As it is, you do not belong to the world, because I have chosen you out of the world. That is why the world hates you" (John 15:18-19). It certainly appears today that Christian churches do not want to be hated, so they try to protect themselves by not preaching against sin. "Blessed are you when people hate you, when they exclude you and insult you and reject your name as evil, because of the Son of Man. Rejoice in that day and leap for joy, because great is your reward in heaven. For that is how their ancestors treated the prophets" (Luke 6:22, 23).

There is a non-Biblical expression concerning love and hate that is frequently heard, and it is: we are to love the sinner, but hate the sin. Although that is not a quote from the Bible, it definitely is the will of God. That is who he is. "But God demonstrates his own love for us in this: While we were still sinners, Christ died for us" (Romans 5:8). "Greater love has no one than this: to lay down one's life for one's friends. You are my friends if you do what I command" (John 15:13). However, regarding the expression: "Love the sinner, hate the sin", there is a problem with the way the expression is sometimes used. To love the sinner is paramount, but it is also important to hate the sin. To tell a sinner, "God loves you" is the truth. It does not matter who the person is, what they have done, or what they are going to do, God loves each person in the world. God loves them so much that he condescended to be born on earth as a man named Jesus, and to willingly

119

give his life's blood on the cross, to pay for the sin of the world. That is how much he loves you. That's how much he loves each and every person. But if we fail to mention, that God hates their sin, we have not shown a love for them, but rather a hatred for them which could send them to hell. By just saying "God loves you." we have in essence told sinner that they are acceptable to God just the way they are. No changes need to be made. God does not have to be recognized, prayed to, or even believed in. You are OK. If we give the sinner confidence in their current state, without explaining that God hates sin and desires that we repent of it, and have it forgiven through faith in Christ, we are not loving them. That would not be love but rather it would be showing a deadly disregard for their eternal life. God loves all the people of the world, but consider, "Enter through the narrow gate. For wide is the gate and broad is the road that leads to destruction, and many enter through it. But small is the gate and narrow the road that leads to life, and only a few find it" (Matthew 7:13, 14). Faith in Jesus is the narrow gate. Jesus is telling us that if we reject God's love for us, expressed through Jesus Christ, then we are the ones who have rejected life and instead we have chosen death. It seems that he is also telling us, that numerically there will be many more who are lost than those who are saved.

Do you still believe that the love of God will save everyone, regardless of their sin? How do you explain Matthew 7:13, 14? How do you explain Genesis chapters 6 and 7 where it is written that the Lord wipes out the entire population of the world, except for Noah, and seven others, because he hated the wickedness of the world? How do you explain the destruction of Sodom and Gomorrah, recorded in Genesis 19? Did not God love the people of Sodom and Gomorrah, but annihilated them because of their wickedness? This is serious. This concerns the eternal life of you, your family and loved ones, and all others. God is love, but if his love, offered to all, in the life, death, and resurrection of Jesus Christ, is refused, then what?

Love the sinner, and tell them that God loves them too, but also explain that the way to life, through faith in Christ Jesus, is to repent, turn from their sin and ask for forgiveness. Faith in Jesus Christ is an attempt to obey him, and when we fail, to ask for forgiveness, and try again.

Love what God loves, and hate what God hates. God loves people and God hates sin.

Still, whoever will, may come.

Directions to Heaven

Chapter 10

Forgiving Others

Why is this such a difficult subject? It is because it goes against our basic sense of justice. If you do something wrong, you must pay. That seems fair. If we have earned our livelihood by the sweat of our brow, then why should we be expected to forgive a thief? This is a simple and understandable example of why we have a problem with forgiving. Countless cowboy movies seen in my childhood were about some bad guy who had done something wrong, and the good guy went after him to make him pay. It was the right thing to do. I refer to it as the John Wayne complex. (Didn't you love John Wayne!) A job well done, and the cowboy and his girl, or sometimes just he and his horse, ride off into the sunset. A happy ending. Problem solved. No forgiveness needed.

If God had looked on our sin in the same way (we are the bad person) then he could have taken care of it by sending us all to hell. Problem solved. No forgiveness needed.

Thank you, Father, for loving sinners in the world so much, that you gave us your only begotten son, that we might be forgiven, and receive life.

The example of what God has done for us is demonstrated in Matthew 18: 23-35. Jesus tells a story of a wealthy king, and a man who owed him ten thousand bags of gold. (Other accounts of this story indicate that whatever the debt was, it was so huge that it was beyond imagination). Since he could not repay, the king ordered that he, his wife and family, and all he owned, be sold to repay the debt. The man pleaded for mercy, and time to repay, and the king took pity on him, and forgave his debt. Then this man who had been forgiven enormously, saw another who owed him a small amount. When that person could not pay, the man who had just been forgiven, had this small debtor thrown into prison. When the king heard of it, he called that servant back in. "You wicked servant," he said, "I canceled all that debt of yours because you begged me to. Shouldn't you have had mercy on your fellow servant just as I had on you?" (Matthew 18:32,33). Then the king handed this fellow over to be tortured until he could pay everything back. Please read the full story in Matthew 18.

Jesus is making it clear. We have no way of paying for our sins. The debt is far beyond our ability to pay. But Jesus has paid the price for us in full. Now do we, in our pride of who we are, and what we think we deserve, have no mercy on those who are indebted to us? This is not just about money. It is about the attitude of our heart, when dealing with others who have wronged us.

Still, there is a practicality in life that tells us, if someone steals your car, call the cops. If someone harms your family, call the cops, etc. Standing for the law, and holding lawbreakers accountable is not in conflict with the practice of forgiving. If you fail to help take a criminal off the streets, and that criminal goes on to harm others, aren't you the one who needs to ask for forgiveness?

The individual problems we have with forgiveness, seem to be without number. I will not try to list them. I will let you do that, since you know more about it than anyone else. Let's start by making it a little easier. Forgiveness is not acceptance. You are not telling a person that what they did is OK. It is not OK. They have broken God's command and have caused injury. Forgiving them is not an endorsement of their wrong. If you are angry over minor offenses, pray that God will give you the healing and the confidence in the Lord, to forgive freely and get past these things. However, at times, the injury caused cannot be repaired. There is no money, there are no words, and there are no deeds that can make it right again. What then? If that is the case, then you are left with the rest of your life, and the question is, what do you desire your life to be, at peace, or in turmoil? Are you seeking vengeance? Remember, the Lord has said: "It is mine to avenge; I will repay," (Deuteronomy 32:35). Will the rest of your life be filled with unforgiving and anger? Will you allow your physical body and your mind to suffer harm, because of your anger? How long will you refuse to forgive? For the rest of your life? If not forgiving causes sleepless nights and causes your stomach and your head to ache, do you feel that is accomplishing something good for you? Will you continue to not forgive them, after you enter heaven? Or do you think that by the time you get to heaven, you will forget about it? What if in about two or three million years, you remember it, and it starts bugging you. Accept the healing from the Lord. Release yourself from bondage. Forgive.

When Jesus from the cross prayed to his Father for those who crucified and insulted him: "Father, forgive them, for they do not know what they are doing" (Luke 23:34). He spoke truth to us, and for us. If we and others really knew who Jesus is, and who the Almighty God is, we would not do the some of the things we do. We would not hold on to the worldly pride of being "in the right" and demanding our due respect. If we had any idea of the enormity of God's grace, and the infinitude of time, we would be more inclined to let go of the things of no value, and even things of great earthly value, to forgive, and trust God. The Lord loves that sinner, and is disappointed because they have harmed you. Pray that the one who wronged you will find peace with God.

This is not an easy problem. This is one of the most difficult problems I know. Difficult, but trust the Lord when he gives you the pathway to peace and healing.

126

Forgive. I can only pray that you will find the peace of God which passes all understanding.

Directions to Heaven

Chapter 11

To Judge or not to Judge

Currently, there are some Christian pastors and teachers who are advocating that certain practices, allowed by our national laws, are sinful practices. They are teaching that these practices are violations of God's law, even though our state and national laws permit them. For example, the practices of homosexuality, same gender marriage, and abortion.

Other Christian pastors and teachers are saying that we must "err on the side of compassion", and not "condemn" those who are no more than sinners, like us. None of us can keep God's law perfectly. Who is right? Is there a right, and consequently, a wrong? Who is able to cast the first stone? Who can judge another brother or sister within God's church, and who can judge another person who is not even a believer in our God.

I have heard it preached that "Judging is from Satan". They say that the practice of passing judgment on another is an act like that of Satan, who himself aspired to set on God's throne and be like God. They say that proper judgment of the individual is to be left to God, and not to be usurped by man. How nice. How compassionate. But is this what God desires of us? Doesn't God want us to be compassionate? Does God demand that we are tolerant of sin, or does God demand that we be compassionate and judge sin for what it is? Does judgment come from our own pride and arrogance? Is our judgment hypocritical?

"Let the message of Christ dwell among you richly as you teach and admonish one another with all wisdom through psalms, hymns, and songs from the Spirit, singing to God with gratitude in your hearts" (Colossians 3:16). The word admonish means to correct, or to express a warning or disapproval, in an earnest and concerned way. In other words, determining a need for correction and addressing it in a loving and thoughtful way. Even though it is loving and concerned, it is making a judgment.

"Hate evil, love good" (Amos 5:15). God has commanded us to do this, and it cannot be done without making a judgment as to what is good and what is evil. Our basis for judging (discerning) is the word of God. This has nothing to do with condemning. We have no power, authority, or desire to condemn anyone.

Why Does God call us to judge each other? The answer is simple, good, and straight forward. God loves us, and wants us to honor and obey him, because the law he has given us is good, and it is for our benefit. An early life example are the laws and instructions that parents give to their children. The laws are not given to restrict the children's happiness, but rather to guide them to have a safe life. When a child is found playing in the street, when that is a violation of the parent's law, the child is punished. Not out of hatred for the child, but because of their love for the child. We are to love each other in the same way. We are obligated to warn others of their mistake. We are not held responsible if they do not take the advice, but we do have the obligation to warn them.

Christians are all too eager to claim verses from the Bible that give them comfort, "For I know the plans I have for you," declares the Lord, "plans to prosper you and not to harm you, plans to give you hope and a future" (Jeremiah 29:11). They frequently ignore verses that call them to service and accountability before God. "Son of man, I have made you a watchman for the people of Israel; so hear the word I speak and give them warning from me. When I say to a wicked person, 'You will surely die,' and you do not warn them or speak out to dissuade them from their evil ways in order to save their life, that wicked person will die for their sin, and I will hold you accountable for their blood. But if you do warn the wicked person and they do not turn from their wickedness or from their evil ways, they will die for their sin; but you will have saved yourself" (Ezekiel 3:17-19).

Is this judgment, or is this merely a loving warning to someone breaking God's law? Read the scripture again. The reason God wants us to warn the wicked person is to save their life. Is that a bad thing, or a loving attitude?

Although this command to Ezekiel was given hundreds of years before, Paul believed it applied to him when he proclaims, "Therefore, I declare to you today that I am innocent of the blood of any of you. For I have not hesitated to proclaim to you the whole will of God" (Acts 20:26,27).

There are times and conditions in this world when proclaiming God's law to a sinner, would be threatening to the evangelist, even to imprisonment or death and in these cases, to the discernment of the individual, I believe there is a reasonable time to be silent. This attitude seems to be instructed by Christ in his sermon on the mount. "Do not give dogs what is sacred; do not throw your pearls to pigs. If you do, they may trample them under their feet, and then turn and tear you to pieces" (Matthew 7:6). But for those of us who know, believe, and love God's word, and his grace, the choice being silent is not always an option. When Jeremiah received the word of the Lord, he probably thought he would be highly respected for proclaiming it. However, to his dismay he found that he was ridiculed and mocked. None the less, when he decided that because of this he would remain silent, he found he could not. "But if I say, 'I will not mention his word or speak any more in his name,' his word is in my heart like a fire, a fire shut up in my bones. I am weary of holding it in, indeed, I cannot" (Jeremiah 20:9).

Verses in the Bible used to teach against judging are often misquoted or taken out of context. The one I've heard misused most often is: "Judge not" (Matthew 7:1 NKJV). Jesus is talking about making hypocritical judgments. He is talking to a hypocrite. In verse 5, Jesus says "You hypocrite," then he goes on to say first take care of your own problem and then you can see clearly to help your brother with his small problem. The admonition here is that he *should* make the judgment of his brothers' minor sin, but make it rightly, not hypocritically, as Jesus said, "Stop judging by mere appearances, but instead judge correctly" (John 7:24). The command is to judge, but do it rightly.

This concept of hypocritical judgment is repeated where Paul says: "You, therefore, have no excuse, you who pass judgment on someone else, for at whatever point you judge the other, you are condemning yourself, because you who pass judgment do the same things" (Romans 2:1). The Wycliffe Bible Commentary explains that scripture this way. "The word judge (*krinon*) occurs three times in verse 1. It means here to pass unfavorable judgment by criticizing or finding fault. The man who is inexcusable is the one who has great power of criticism but no self-discipline." [1]

An example of what is meant by these passages in Matthew and Romans would be, don't rebuke your brother for his involvement in pornography, while you yourself are in an adulterous relationship. First get yourself right with

God. Stop your sin, repent, and pray for forgiveness. After healing your problem, then you will be better able to council others, and through your (loving) judging and admonishing you might help them to draw nearer to the Lord.

Some verses imply that Paul taught against judging, but nothing could be farther from the truth. Read about Paul's judgment of a church member who was committing a vile sin while being a member of the Corinthian church. Paul proclaimed, "Even though I am not physically present, I am with you in spirit. As one who is present with you in this way, I have already passed judgment in the name of our Lord Jesus on the one who has been doing this" (1 Corinthians 5:3). Further in this passage he says, "What business is it of mine to judge those outside the church? Are you not to judge those inside? God will judge those outside. Expel the wicked person from among you" (1 Corinthians 5:12,13). Paul makes it clear that we are to judge those inside the church, and expel any member who will not live according to God's commands. Even so, most believe that the person was cast out, is the same person who in 2 Corinthians 2:5-8, is deemed by Paul to have been punished enough and should be brought back into fellowship.

This is a beautiful example of the purpose in judging. To give assistance in correcting our mistakes, and re-establish good relationships between each other and with God.

This is also what James was talking about, "Whoever turns a sinner from the error of their way will save them from death and cover over a multitude of sins" (James 5:20). How else could this be done except to judge the sinner of his sin, and encourage them to repent.

Paul's comment "I care very little if I am judged by you or by any human court; indeed, I do not even judge myself" (1 Corinthians 4:3) is clearly referring to, and only referring to his faithfulness in being a servant of Christ and being entrusted with the secret things of God, as he explains in verses 1 and 2. The valid judgment of this matter is left only to God. However, on other matters of sin or shortcoming in his life, Paul is a very critical judge of himself as is evidenced in Romans chapter 7. All of us saved by the grace of God struggle with our failure to be perfect. We have sins of commission, sins of omission, failures and shortcomings that sadden us from time to time as we ask for forgiveness and the chance to try again. After Paul's admission that he does what he should not do, and does not do what he should, he first expresses his dilemma, and then answers his own question: "O wretched man that I am! Who will deliver me from this body of death? I thank God — through Jesus Christ our Lord!" (Romans 7:24,25 NKJV). This is an expression and an attitude we frequently share with him.

As far as Paul's previous statement "What business is it of mine to judge those outside the church?" Obviously the church has no authority over non-members, they cannot be expelled, they are not even a member. This passage is about discipline within the church, and as punishment for the violation of church standards, there was the loss of fellowship. The church has no power of discipline over the non-member, and to threaten those outside the church with the loss of fellowship would be meaningless.

A better and more complete example of our judging people outside the church can be seen in the life of John the Baptist. His open and repeated judging and rebuking of Herod the tetrarch, cost him his life. He not only judged and openly rebuked his political leader, accusing him of adultery with his brother's wife, but in Luke 3:19 he rebuked Herod for "all of all the other evil things he had done." This guy would not shut up. He saw God's law being broken and he had to confront the one breaking it. Even if it was Herod. What do you think Jesus would think of someone who judged and rebuked others so harshly? Jesus tells us his answer. After Herod had John arrested and placed in prison, and before John was murdered by decapitation, Jesus said of him, "Truly I tell you, among those born of women there has not risen anyone greater than John the Baptist" (Matthew 11:11).

When Jesus confronted the woman caught in adultery, he told her, "Then neither do I condemn you," Jesus declared. "Go now and leave your life of sin" (John 8:11). Jesus did not come into the world to condemn the world, but that the world through him might be saved.

(See John 3:17). Jesus did not condemn her, but he did judge her to be guilty of sin and told her to leave it.

Making judgments is everyday life. Those of us who believe in the Lord Jesus are tempted throughout our lives with sinful choices. We must judge right from wrong, good from evil, and make our choices. When we make a mistake, God desires that we repent, because he loves us. When we see others making bad choices, we should warn them. That is not condemning, but it is judging or at least discerning and counseling. It is because of the love we have for them, and the faith we have in God, that after making a godly judgment, we warn them.

Directions to Heaven

Chapter 12

Nicer Than God

God is truth. If we disagree with God, we lie.

Recently, I heard a most interesting thought. Today we have many questions for the Lord. We want to know why is there evil. Why doesn't Jesus return and claim the victory he has already won. Why will Satan be released from the Abyss after one thousand years. And many other questions. The answer usually given before has been: When we get to heaven God will explain it to us. The recent thought I heard expressed was: When we are changed, leaving the mortal, and taking on the immortal, we will be like Jesus. At that time, we will not have to ask questions, rather we will see things as God sees them, and we will know that everything God has done, and all that he has allowed to happen has been perfect. "Dear friends, now we are children of God, and what we will be has not yet been made known. But we know that when Christ appears, we shall be like him, for we shall see him as he is" (1 John 3:2).

"VATICAN CITY (AP) — Pope Francis has decreed that the death penalty is 'inadmissible' under all circumstances and the Catholic Church should campaign to abolish it, a change in church teaching that could influence Catholic politicians and judges in the US and across the globe. The change, announced Thursday, was hailed by anti-death penalty activists, and scorned by Francis' frequent conservative critics, who said he had no right to change what Scripture revealed and popes have taught for centuries. The Vatican said that Francis had amended the Catechism of the Catholic Church — the compilation of official Catholic teaching — to say that capital punishment can never be sanctioned because it constitutes an "attack" on the dignity of human beings." [1]

— —

"And for your lifeblood I will surely demand an accounting. I will demand an accounting from every animal. And from each human being, too, I will demand an accounting for the life of another human being. 'Whoever sheds human blood, by humans shall their blood be shed; for in the image of God has God made mankind"
(Genesis 9:5, 6).

Is the Pope being nicer than God? Does the Pope show mercy where the Almighty God has hardness of heart?

The Catechism says:

#882 "For the Roman Pontiff, by reason of his office as Vicar of Christ, and as pastor of the entire Church has full, supreme, and universal power over the whole Church, a power which he can always exercise unhindered."

#2034 "The Roman Pontiff and the bishops are 'authentic teachers, that is, teachers endowed with the authority of Christ, who preach the faith to the people entrusted to them, the faith to be believed and put into practice.' The ordinary and universal magisterium of the Pope and the bishops in communion with him teach the faithful the truth to believe, the charity to practice, the beatitude to hope for."

Magisterium: The claim of the Roman Catholic Church that they and they alone, through the Pope and his Bishops have the authorization and power to teach religious truth.

The term Vicar, is from the Latin word: *vicarius*, meaning: substitute, or in the place of. So, the Popes of the Roman Catholic Church have substituted for, and are serving in the place of Jesus himself. However, because of the long, long, long line of Catholic Popes, whose lives of murder, avarice, depravity, pride, debauchery, and evil is

141

well documented in the book *A Woman Rides the Beast*[2], by Dave Hunt, the idea of Popes being the actual presence of Jesus Christ on this earth is ludicrous. If you should believe that Mr. Hunt's depiction of the history of the Roman Catholic Church, and its Vicars of Christ to be too condemning, and suspect it is because Dave Hunt is not a Catholic, but speaking poorly of the Catholics, then might I suggest you examine a similar record of the Pope's degeneracy through the centuries as reported by Malachi Martin in his book, *The Decline and Fall of the Roman Church*[3]. Malachi Martin is a former Jesuit and professor who served in Rome with Cardinal Augustine Bea and Pope John XXIII.

If you are a Christian, then you probably believe as I do that the Bible is not only the best but is the only authoritative source of written truth, from God. It explains who he is, what he has done, and how he has created and engaged with mankind. No one has the authority from God to change it.

I recall, few decades ago, there was a magazine company that also published condensed books. In fact, I have read some of their condensed books and found them to be well done, and quite enjoyable. However, when they decided to condense the Bible, that to me was unacceptable. After all, if this is God's truth, who on earth can say that part of it is unnecessary? I heard they omitted the verses which state: "I warn everyone who hears the words of the prophecy of this scroll: If anyone adds anything to them, God will add to that person the plagues described in this scroll. And if anyone takes words away from this scroll of prophecy, God will take away from that person any share in the tree of life and in the holy city, which are described in this scroll" (Revelation 22:18,19).

God is eternal. God's word is eternal. "The grass withers and the flowers fall, but the word of our God stands forever" (Isaiah 40:8).

Many of our Christian denominations have denied the truth of God in scripture, and tried to be "nicer than God". When God defines adultery, fornication, lying, stealing, sexual immorality, and other acts to be sinful, but churches, denominations, or individuals, declare those sins to be acceptable, they are not being nicer than God, they are lying, and leading people to death. Christian churches should not arrogantly proclaim their rebellion against God, by condoning that which God himself has condemned. However, the falling away of so many churches could be the rebellion soon to occur. (See 2 Thessalonians 2:1–3). These verses speak of the rebellion, the falling away from truth, that must occur before the "day of the Lord" that is the great tribulation.

Sin can be forgiven. In Christ alone, there can be forgiveness of sin, however I know of no place in the Bible where acts that the Lord declares to be sinful, are ever considered to be acceptable. When clergy are known to have sexually molested children in their care, don't you

143

know that God hates that. And when these crimes are left unresolved and the criminals left unpunished, don't you know that God is angered? Is it not like the time when Paul rebuked the Jews who claimed to be God's own, but who were known to have violated God's law? "You, then who teach others, do you not teach yourself? You who preach against stealing, do you steal? You who say that people should not commit adultery, do you commit adultery? You who abhor idols, do you rob temples? You who brag about the law, do you dishonor God by breaking the law? As it is written: 'God's name is blasphemed among the Gentiles because of you'" (Romans 2:21-24). When those who claim to be representing Jesus, violate God's law, don't Christians and non-Christians alike notice, and consider their religion to be a lie, and to be worthless? And don't others feel justified in blaspheming our God because of our duplicity? We must say: "Let God be true, and every human being a liar" (Romans 3:4).

One of my favorite verses is: "Or do you not know that wrongdoers will not inherit the kingdom of God? Do not be deceived: Neither the sexually immoral nor idolaters nor adulterers nor men who have sex with men nor thieves nor the greedy nor drunkards nor slanderers nor swindlers will inherit the kingdom of God. And that is what some of you were. But you were washed, you were sanctified, you were justified in the name of the Lord Jesus Christ and by the Spirit of our God" (1 Corinthians 6:9-11). What I really love about this scripture is the fact that Paul points out "That is what some of you were." All of us are sinners, and as such will not enter the kingdom of heaven, unless we come to Jesus Christ for the forgiveness of and cleansing away of our sin. If we do, then our sin is canceled and paid for, and we who *were* the vilest of sinners can be justified, and sanctified. It is this status of believers in Christ that avails for us the grace of God, to eternal salvation. After having received this salvation by the grace of God, all of us will continue to have sin in our lives, of some kind, to some degree, but as long as we agree with God that we have sinned, repent, and confess our sin to him, we will remain forgiven, and cleansed by his blood. "If we confess our sins, he is faithful and just and will forgive us our sins and purify us from all unrighteousness" (1John 1:9). John was talking to his brothers in Christ. He said, "My dear children, I write this to you so that you will not sin. But if anybody does sin, we have an advocate with the Father – Jesus Christ, the Righteous One" (1 John 2:1).

We cannot be nicer than God, by declaring sin to be acceptable, or in changing God's law. That is not being nice, but rather that is lying and leading the unwary to death.

God is good. His law is perfect. His law is our blessed instruction. Do not think that you can be nicer than God.

Directions to Heaven

Chapter 13

Put into Practice

When people visit a museum, they are frequently impressed with the beauty of the artwork by the old masters, and many artists who were previously unknown to them. The museum's quality paintings are explained to them by the curator or an assistant who is well versed in classic art. See the beautiful expressions, the eyes, how lifelike, the use of light and contrasting darkness. See the expressions on the faces, and the superb manor of the blending brush strokes. We have a sense of awe at the talent that some people have. But then we leave, and go about our way, and the motivation of our lives has not been changed.

Regrettably, that is the way many sermons are received in American churches today. We hear the message, we understand the point, and agree with it, then go our way for the more important things like lunch, and the game to follow. Where is the conviction? Where is the evidence of a life changed by faith in the word of the Lord God Almighty? Where is the instruction and admonition to identify and turn from the sins in our lives, which are rampant in our country today? Where the call to repentance? Where is the call to service? Are we only to be told how much God loves us, and that we are to have a nice day? Where is the calling to be a witness for Jesus Christ in a country that is trying to make Jesus Christ illegal? Where is the fervent call to believe and be baptized for the salvation of your eternal life? Fortunately, it is not all frivolous. Many times in churches and in the sermons of their faithful pastors, we are still receiving good instruction to believe, to give our lives to Christ for salvation and to live and do the will of God. We can't read scripture without being convicted to live for the Lord. Still, it seems that so many churches have turned away from sound doctrine. Beware: "My people come to you as they usually do, and sit before you to hear your words, but they do not put them into practice. With their mouths they speak of love, but their hearts are greedy for unjust gain. Indeed, to them you are nothing more than one who sings love songs with a beautiful voice and plays an instrument well, for they hear your words but do not put them into practice" (Ezekiel 33:31,32). It's just like visiting a museum.

When studying about the rapture, that is quickly approaching, a warning about the time prior to the rapture is that there will be rebellion, or the time of apostasy. This rebellion is a major falling away from faith in Jesus Christ. It will be a major falling away from the doctrinal positions once believed in. Could this desire of churches and denominations to declare that sinfulness is acceptable, and the steady decline of church attendance be the prophesied rebellion? The government has power to establish policies which encourage freedom of religion, or to place restrictions on it. Our own government can demand that we deny what God has commanded us to obey. Wherever Satan can drive a wedge between people and God, expect him to be there.

Do you think that just by appearing in church, you show others that you are holy? "Will you steal and murder, commit adultery and perjury, burn incense to Baal and follow other gods you have not known, and then come and stand before me in this house, which bears my Name, and say, 'We are safe' — safe to do all these detestable things? Has this house, which bears my Name, become a den of robbers to you? But I have been watching! Declares the Lord" (Jeremiah 7:9-11). We are deceived, not God. "Do not be deceived: God cannot be mocked. A man reaps what he sows" (Galatians 6:7).

"Therefore everyone who hears these words of mine and puts them into practice is like a wise man who built his house on the rock. The rain came down, the streams rose, and the winds blew and beat against that house; yet it did not fall, because it had its foundation on the rock. But everyone who hears these words of mine and does not put them into practice is like a foolish man who built his house on sand. The rain came down, the streams rose, and the winds blew and beat against that house, and it fell with a great crash" (Matthew 7:24-27). Jesus said this at the end of his Sermon on the Mount, which is recorded in Matthew chapters 5-7. Are you building on the rock? Are you putting his words into practice? In Matthew 5, Are you

149

blessed in the beatitudes listed in Matthew 5:1-11. Do you see yourself in the similitudes? Are you the salt of the earth? Are you the light of the world? Do you heed the instruction "Do not merely listen to the word, and so deceive yourselves. Do what it says" (James 1: 22). Jesus said: "Whoever has my commands and obeys them, he is the one who loves me" (John 14:21). "If anyone loves me, he will obey my teachings" (John14:23). Do you depend on your faith in Jesus Christ so that God will grant you his grace? If you have faith in him, you will obey his commands. What commands, you ask? Love the Lord your God with all your heart, love your neighbor as you do yourself. Obey the commandments of the law and teach them. Forgive. Do not lust or act on lust. Do not swear by anything. Do not lie. God hates lies. Store up your treasures in heaven, where your heart is. Seek first the kingdom of God and his righteousness. Do not judge hypocritically, judge rightly. Live the golden rule. Know the words of Christ and put them into practice. Go into the harvest fields (Witness). Be shrewd as snakes but as innocent (harmless) as doves. Acknowledge Christ before men. Do not love anyone or anything more than Christ. When it comes to obeying the laws of God, they are many and varied. Some seem to be far more important than others, but I believe that the law of God is singular. This is confirmed by James 2:10 "For whoever keeps the whole law and yet stumbles at just one point is guilty of breaking all of it." This is somewhat like the following picture. Imagine that our perfect God is in heaven, and in his hand is a beautiful circle of pure crystal. Let's call that first crystal, the first commandment. Looped through that first crystal is a second circle of crystal. Call this the second commandment. These interlocking circles of perfect crystal continue, one for each law, each command, each precept, through space, down to you. Picture yourself holding on to the last crystal circle, as you are supported over the lake of fire. Now then, which of these individual crystal circles, representing the laws of God, do you think it would be OK to break? It would be best to stop this analogy here, before it sounds too much like the great sermon of Jonathan Edwards, "Sinners in the hands of an angry God". We all have sinned, and we all do sin. Praise be to God, we have a savior who has paid the price for our sin. After coming in faith to Jesus, there is the process called sanctification, being set apart from the world (worldly values). This process, which is "putting into practice" the law of God, leads to holiness. Even though we are to grow toward holiness, the word holy is so majestic and is so descriptive of the Lord, that we cannot fully attain it until we see him as he is, and become like him. (See 1 John 3:2) Thank you Lord for sending your Son to save us from all our sins. Loving and obeying God's law is not legalism! You are saved by grace alone, by faith alone! Works provide no salvation. But if you believe, you will do them, because they prove your faith. You will do them because they honor God, and because of your love for Christ causes you to enjoy doing things which you know please him, and bring honor to him, and you will love these things that he loves. And, by the way, for those of us who most properly are interested in laying up for ourselves, treasures in heaven, this is a good way to do it. If you think your 401 is something of value, you had better be increasing the value of your "For ol' 1". Things done for God have eternal value.

Repenting

This should be a continuing practice in every Christian's life. There is no greater release from the guilt and burden of sin, and it is followed by a blessed peace of mind. When we take a bath or shower, we clean away the outside grime and stain that accumulates. When we spend time in prayer, repenting of our failure to be perfect, we cleanse our soul of all the guilty stains. This leaves us with the incredible peace of God that passes all understanding. Don't deny yourself this regular refreshing of the soul.

Chapter 14

Politics for the Christian

How does a Christian honor God with their political attitudes, comments, and votes?

First things first. The question is asked about a particular type of person. A Christian. I am defining a Christian to be a person who believes that Jesus is our savior from God, who is God, and was the Word incarnate. Who by shedding his life's blood voluntarily on Calvary's cross, was dead and buried, was bodily resurrected, and has paid the price for the sin of the world, so that whoever believes in him will be saved from Hell. For this discussion, that is a Christian.

There are people in the USA who call themselves Christian, by the above definition, but who do not vote in political elections. It may very well be that they do not vote specifically because they are Christian, and they are of the opinion, I'm going to leave everything to God.

That reminds me of the story of a man whose house was engulfed by flood waters. As the waters rose and came up to his front porch, a neighbor arrived in a rowboat and offered to row the man to a safe location, but the man replied, "I'm depending on the Lord to save me." Later that day when the water had risen higher, and he was standing on a balcony, a motorboat came by and offered to save him, but his reply was the same, "I'm depending on the Lord to save me." Finally, as he stood on the roof, a helicopter hovered over him and offered to take him to safety, but the man was resolute in his faith, "I'm depending on the Lord to save me." When the waters continued their rise, the man was drowned. Being a Christian, his soul went to heaven, where he saw the Lord face to face. So disappointed that his faith in God had not been rewarded, he asked: "Why did you not answer my prayer to be saved?" The Lord said: "I answered it three times, and each time you refused it." You see, that person was given the opportunity to choose life, but chose to ignore it. In politics, God has given you the opportunity to choose life. To ignore it is a choice for death. You yourself may very well go to heaven, but why cause death of country and countrymen by not voting to elect political representatives who support righteousness and oppose wickedness.

In this country, our founding fathers who established this nation in the name of God and our savior Jesus Christ, (See the many, many founding documents.) have given us the power to choose our political leaders. In this nation, just like Israel (See the Bible, 1 and 2 Kings, 1 and 2 Chronicles, etc.) we have had good and godly leaders, and we have had evil ones. Even though you and I might differ on who was good, or bad, you know we have had both.

When you as a Christian, refuse to vote, and refuse to choose good over evil when you are given the opportunity to do so, then you should not pray to God and ask him to give us good leaders. He gave you the opportunity to honor him, and you refused.

To listen to many a politician, the truth is difficult to find and evaluate. Speeches are positive and promising, and add campaigns, at least some of the positive ones, sound as good as advertisements for a new breakfast cereal. There are many subtleties. However, it is not the subtleties that we need to be concerned with. It is the gross, blatant, egregious violations of our belief that must be addressed. There is only one source of truth which tells us about our God and what he commands of us, and that is the Bible. The New Testament, and the Old Testament. The entire Bible which is our source of knowing God, and knowing his will. When a politician votes to take the Bible out of schools, Christians should vote that politician out of office. When God calls life, made in his image, precious, and politicians vote to end life in the mother's womb, Christians should vote that politician out of office. When God establishes marriage to be between a man and a woman, the basis of family, and a politician votes to destroy it, Christians should vote that politician out of office. How can you disagree with these matters, without proclaiming that you are the one who decides right and

155

wrong, and your opinion is more valuable than God's decree.

Don't leave good seed in the sack to rot, plant it. Express your opinion. In your daily conversation, sow the seeds of your godly opinions, so people can hear some good news. If you and I are Christian, we still might choose different candidates. We still might take different sides of any particular debate. But each of us is obligated before God to vote to bring forth what is good, to the best of our own determination. There are many political issues which you have been repeatedly given the opportunity to vote on, either directly or by knowing the preferences of the politicians who are running for office. How about allowing the Bible in schools? Is that not an issue you have an opinion on? Don't you have a preference? If other religions can be explained to school children and young adults, why not Christianity, which is unquestionably the foundation of our country. Vote for it. Vote for candidates who support prayer, in Jesus' name. We have already had evil people in this country diminish our freedom of speech, (political correctness, hate speech) and our freedom of religion (restrictions against praying in Jesus' name in schools, even in the military). Vote against politicians who support abortion. Foundationally, read and know your Bible. A deplorable fact is that many people who call themselves Christian do not know the Bible. I have talked with several who are satisfied to be "Christian", or think that they are Christian, because they are church members, or they have gone to church and because of that, believe they have the gift of grace, but still have no interest in reading, much less in knowing the Bible. How can anyone say that Jesus is God, who came to earth to die for me so I might have eternal life, and in the next breath say they are not interested enough in him to even read what he said. Incredible.

Over a period of many, many decades, through apathy and disinterest, we have allowed the disintegration of the laws that have given us guidance and protection. Bit by bit our laws and standards have been attacked and chipped away. The laws and Christian mores which gave us direction, that guided us in the right, and that protected us, have been chipped away. It seems like the condition of the city of Jerusalem, during the time of Ezra and Nehemiah. The temple had been destroyed, the walls were down, and the city gates had been burned. Nehemiah desperately desired for his city to be reestablished, and he knew that could not be done unless the temple was rebuilt, and the walls repaired, and the city gates replaced. That is how the United States is today. The laws and standards that we once had, the standards that truly made us a Christian nation are in disrepair, due to disinterest, and attack. Be an Ezra. Rebuild the temple of your faith. Be a Nehemiah, and rebuild the walls of your country.

God has given us the opportunity to choose. You are responsible for choosing. When Moses talked to the people, he told them that it was a choice that they, individually must make. "This day I call heaven and earth as witnesses against you that I have set before you life and death, blessings and curses. Now choose life, so that you and your children may live and that you may love the Lord your God, listen to his voice, and hold fast to him" (Deuteronomy 30:19, 20). Moses was telling the people to choose to love God and hold fast to him. Today, in political elections, we have that opportunity to choose. Do not allow death and curses by your failure to vote, choose life and blessings. Vote!

Chapter 15

Lying

I will start by giving you the truth about lies. Truth is life, lies are death.

What is a lie? If I say something that is not true, is that a lie? Well, not necessarily. A lie is the presentation of incorrect information, which the presenter knows is incorrect, and they make the false statement for the express purpose to deceive. A statement that is not true could be because of ignorance. One might think they are being truthful, but they are mistaken. Sometimes false statements are made in humor. "I just caught a fish that was so big, that it swallowed the boat and I had to swim back to shore. The statement is untrue, but I doubt if anyone will be deceived. Another kind of condition might occur when a wife asks her husband, "Does this dress make me look fat?". If the husband answers "No my dear, you look as beautiful as ever." Has he lied? Assuming that the dress does seem to increase her heft. One interpretation of the facts might reveal that the husband believes that his wife is really asking him, "Do you still love me?" And by saying, "you are as beautiful as ever." he has in fact answered truthfully, "Yes my dear wife, I still love you." I'm not a lawyer, but I don't see enough evidence here to hold this over for trial, case dismissed.

Lies of the deceitful variety are rampant in our society today. Television and movies give endless examples of how, being able to lie successfully, is a good and clever talent. Lying is evident in places where it should never be. Lies are frequently in the news as it is printed and spoken. There are people in government who lie. People in all offices and departments who have been elected, and those who were not elected. They corrupt justice for political and personal gain. There are lies in business. There are even lies in the church, in fact some churches are based on lies. At least that is my opinion. It is also my opinion that the determination of truth for the church, and for the individual, is the examination of what the Holy Bible declares to be the truth. Disagreements with this standard is what I am referring to as a lie in the church. There is the corruption of lying all through the lives of people, just as it was in the time of Jeremiah. "From the least to the greatest, all are greedy for gain; prophets and priests alike, all practice deceit. They dress the wound of my people as though it were not serious. 'Peace, peace,' they say, when there is no peace. Are they ashamed of their detestable conduct? No, they have no shame at all; they do not even know how to blush. So they will fall among the fallen; they will be brought down when I punish them," says the Lord" (Jeremiah 6:13-15).

Many times, lies are referred to in the Bible. They are associated with evil and wickedness, and they are never considered clever.

The first evil on earth, recorded in the Bible is when Satan calls God, a liar. Satan asked Eve: Can you not eat of the fruit of the garden? Eve answered, yes we can, but God did say not to eat the fruit from the tree in the middle of the garden, or we will surely die. Satan responded; you will not surely die. Satan, a liar, and the father of lies, tells Eve that God, had told her a lie. This is the first evil recorded in the Bible. See Genesis 3:1-4. We see this character called the serpent, from Genesis to Revelation. In Revelation chapter 20 he is identified as the dragon, that ancient serpent, the devil, and as Satan. Jesus refers to his character more completely by explaining: "He was a murderer from the beginning, not holding to the truth, for there is no truth in him. When he lies, he speaks his native language, for he is a liar and the father of lies" (John 8:44).

God is truth. "Jesus answered, 'I am the way and the truth and the life" John 14:6. So Jesus, who is God, and always has been God, is truth and life.

So, God is truth and life. Satan is lies and death.

We definitely lost something of value in this country when the courts stopped swearing in witnesses by asking them to testify the truth, the whole truth, and nothing but the truth, so help them God. Just another chipping away from our foundation, showing that we as a nation have not fought to maintain what once was a continuing reminder of our obligation to be truthful before God.

The ninth commandment and Proverbs 6:17 and 6:19 confirm God's hatred of lying.

Lies are not clever, funny, or useful. Lies are death.

"The arrogant cannot stand in your presence. You hate all who do wrong; you destroy those who tell lies" (Psalms 5:5,6).

"Whoever of you loves life and desires to see many good days, keep your tongue from evil and your lips from telling lies" (Psalms 34:12,13).

"Even from birth the wicked go astray; from the womb they are wayward, spreading lies" (Psalms 58:3).

"A false witness will not go unpunished, and whoever pours out lies will perish" (Proverbs 19:9).

"Truthful lips endure forever,
but a lying tongue lasts only a moment" (Proverbs 12:19).

"The Lord detests lying lips,
but he delights in people who are trustworthy"
(Proverbs 12:22).

"But the cowardly, the unbelieving, the vile, the murderers, the sexually immoral, those who practice magic arts, the idolaters, and all liars—they will be consigned to the fiery lake of burning sulfur. This is the second death" (Revelation 21:8). *And all liars.*

God hates lies.

Directions to Heaven

Chapter 16

Swearing

May the words of my mouth and
the meditation of my heart
be pleasing in your sight,
Lord, my Rock and
my Redeemer.
(Psalms 19:14)

Once I heard a sermon on the power of the tongue. How we can heal and give life, or we can destroy and bring death, just by the words, tone, and feeling we use to communicate with others. He spoke of the difficulty we have in controlling the tongue. When he spoke on swearing, I felt that he was speaking to me personally. This is something that I became very good at, during the twenty-five years that I was away from the church. Since returning to Christ, dramatically and dynamically in 1977, it was something that had been greatly lessened, but it continued to hang on. He told us something that I had known for years. We have the power and the ability to stop it if we really want to. This power is evidenced in the fact that we, as Christians, do not swear in church. We do not swear in the presence of those whom we know would be greatly offended. At these times we can refrain. I agreed with his thinking, and concluded that I did not swear when I was in the presence of someone who would be offended because I respected them. But then I began to realize that this wasn't the truth. Since I am a Christian, I have been filled with the Holy Spirit, and this member of the Godhead is with me always. Why is it that I think I don't swear when I am in the presence of the pastor, or some dear saintly lady, but would freely swear profanely in the presence of God, who is with me always. Who do I respect? The realization came to me that I did not refrain from swearing because I was showing deference to someone present, but rather, the motive for my not swearing was to conceal from those around me, my true identity. I did not want certain people to know that I was profane. I wanted those people to think highly of me, and to believe that I too was a saintly person. So, the reason I refrained from swearing, in front of some people, was to deceive them, and lie about my own character. Then, when I was alone, and angry, or proud, or when I was driving, or when I was listening to talk radio, or when I was watching sports, or playing sports, or when, or when, or when . . . I would allow a word, or an oath, or on occasion, the blue streak of profanity. Amazingly, I tried to defend myself before God by claiming that the purpose of a language was communication. And I was just expressing my discontent. I have a sufficient vocabulary to use euphemisms, but if I do, I feel that I have not communicated. I can call a person a blaggard, or a blatherskite, or a rapscallion but if I do, I haven't communicated. But if I call him a **&%!+*& then he gets the message, and I feel that I have accurately communicated. This is an unacceptable defense for anyone, especially anyone like me who reads, loves, and believes God's word. I know the passage in the sermon on the mount, where Jesus says: "But let your 'Yes' be 'Yes', and your 'No,' 'No.' For whatever is more than these is from the evil one" (Matthew 5:37 NKJV). I also remember the words of Jesus when he said: "But I say to you that for every idle word men may speak, they will give account of it in the day of judgment." (Matthew 12:36 NKJV). How will you get around that?

Why do we swear? It is to give emphasis. It is to proclaim that we are someone to be reckoned with, that we have power and authority. You mess with me, and you are making a mistake. I have the power, and you had better tremble. Oh? Really? And just where do we get that power and authority? From God? Not too likely. Probably from our own empty sense of pride. Where is the humility? "Pride goes before destruction, a haughty spirit before a fall" (Prov. 16:18). "For all those who exalt themselves will be humbled, and those who humble themselves will be exalted" (Luke 18:14).

"Those who consider themselves religious and yet do not keep a tight rein on their tongues deceive themselves, their religion is worthless" (James 1:26).

167

With our false pride and false authority, we exalt ourselves and make our proclamations for all to hear. Believe me, God hears.

Chapter 17

Barriers

Does your church have greeters? Of course, it does (probably). But whether or not, you no doubt have some practice of welcoming members and especially newcomers.

In several of the churches where I have either had a membership, or was a regular attendee, while I was making up my mind, I have observed the same practice. The superficial practice of welcoming people into your church, but not into your predetermined cliques. You glad hand everyone, and say: "Welcome, it's good to see you here!" Then what? "Hi! It's good to see you!", (sit over there). You are most welcome in their church, but unless you qualify with, the right income, the right level of intellect, the right marital status, living in the right neighborhood, having the right friends already established to recommend you, and bring you in, the welcome is shallow. Frequently you must also qualify by having the right color or ethnicity, or you will be welcome in the church, but don't expect anyone to talk with you or invite you to dinner to find out who you really are. It's just a matter of "Hi, good to see you! (Sit over there).

One of the churches where I was a member, I remember calling a man who was in my Sunday School (Men's Bible Study Class, where I was the teacher) who had dropped out of the class, and had left the church. I called him to ask him why he left, and he answered, "No one would talk with me." There was another lady, an old family friend that I had brought to that church, who left for the same reason. After teaching for two years, and chairing a committee to determine whether or not to hire a new assistant pastor, I left the church for the same reason. I was accepted to teach and serve, and frequently called on to pray, but other than that, I had no friends there, and no one would talk with me.

Another time in another church, a Bible study group I was in, had a new member who was quite intelligent, but acted somewhat differently. I knew he needed a friend, but I left that to someone else. I knew he had struggles with mental health. He left the class and the church by committing suicide. Had I shown an interest in him, it might have made a difference. I don't know that, but strongly suspect that it would have. I know that if I had befriended him, just a little, my own conscience would not now be so burdened as I remember needing to get home to watch the game, rather than inviting him to lunch.

Don't think that your church does not have this problem. It does. That's who we are, unless you are one of those special, extraordinary people who loves God, and loves people. If so, God bless you, as I know he already has. For the rest of us, it is time to make an assessment of what is valuable and what is not. A great way to show our love of God is to give up our comfortable routine, to show regard for someone else. And we should also examine whether we obey God's greatest commandment, or not. "The most important one," answered Jesus, "is this: 'Hear, O Israel: The Lord our God, the Lord is one. Love the Lord your God with all your heart and with all your soul and with all your mind and with all your strength.' The second is this: Love your neighbor as yourself.' There is no commandment greater than these." (Mark 12:29-31).

Directions to Heaven

Chapter 18

About Judas

Judas is not an example of a Christian, who lost his salvation. Judas, although he was one of the original twelve disciples, never was a believer in Jesus Christ. He is a most valuable warning for us today, showing that a person can hear the truth, and see the truth, and be exposed to God himself, and still walk away without believing. A person can even serve in the ministry of Christ, and not be a believer. "'The Spirit gives life; the flesh counts for nothing. The words I have spoken to you — they are full of the Spirit and life. Yet there are some of you who do not believe.' For Jesus had known from the beginning which of them did not believe and who would betray him" (John 6:63, 64). Moments later, "Then Jesus replied, 'Have I not chosen you, the Twelve? Yet one of you is a devil!' (he meant Judas, the son of Simon Iscariot, who, though one of the Twelve, was later to betray him)" (John 6:70, 71).

Another scripture which shows that Judas did not believe that Jesus was the Son of God is: "When Judas, who had betrayed him, saw that Jesus was condemned, he was seized with remorse and returned the thirty pieces of

silver to the chief priests and the elders. 'I have sinned,' he said, 'for I have betrayed innocent blood'"
(Matthew 27:3 ,4). Judas did not say that he had betrayed the Son of God, or the Messiah, or the Christ, but only that he had betrayed innocent blood. He considered Jesus to be just another person who had been unjustly accused.

The death of Judas is recorded in Matthew 27:5 "So Judas threw the money into the temple and left. Then he went away and hanged himself." His death is also recorded in Acts 1:18 "With the payment he received for his wickedness, Judas bought a field; there he fell headlong, his body burst open and all his intestines spilled out." Is there a conflict here? Not necessarily. Have you ever seen anyone fall headlong onto a field? I have. I have seen it thousands of times, and never did their bodies burst open and their intestines spill out. They have even fallen down forcefully, being smashed by some 300 pound tackle, or crushed by a speeding 230 pound linebacker. And never did their intestines spill out. I have been a fan of football since I was big enough to see over the dining room table. I recall seeing some of the old black and white movies about Knute Rockne and Notre Dame, and one about the Army football team with Doc Blanchard and Glenn Davis. I was also a fanatical follower of pro football, up until a few years ago, when I decided there were better ways to spend my time than to watch performers who chose to insult the country I love. Back to Judas. A dead body was a thing to be avoided. It was to be shunned because of the laws of cleanliness, and because a hanging dead body was accursed by God, and people tried to avoid it. "If a man has committed a sin deserving of death, and he is put to death, and you hang him on a tree, his body shall not remain overnight on the tree, but you shall surely bury him that day, so that you do not defile the land which the Lord your God is giving you as an inheritance; for he who is hanged is accursed of God" (Deuteronomy 21:22, 23 NKJV). Who will care for this accursed dead body of Judas, hanging from a tree? No one. The Jews of the Temple wanted nothing to do with him. He had no close family to care for him. He had betrayed Jesus and so had also betrayed the disciples, so they would not show loving compassion for him, and remove his body for burial. No one would care for him and take down his body. It is possible that his body hung there indefinitely until becoming rotted, bloated, and putrefied, and such a repulsive and odoriferous horror that it had to be removed by some low-ranking city official. It is not hard to imagine that on having cut the rope, the decayed and decomposed body fell headlong in the field, bursting open, and his intestines spilling out. Sometimes when there seems to be a discrepancy, it could be that we just do not have all the information. I'm not saying that I know what happened, I don't know, because the information is not given. But there are possibilities.

Chapter 19

Prayer

A young girl had been taught to pray each night, before going to sleep. The prayer was the "standard" now I lay me down to sleep. This was repeated night after night, week, and month. One morning the mother asked, "Did you say your prayer last night." The daughter hesitated and then said: "I thought the Lord might be tired of hearing the same thing every night, so I told him the story of the three bears". I'm sure the Lord was delighted. After all, doesn't he care more about having us share with him, what's on our mind, rather than what you memorized, and can repeat without much thought or feeling?

Prayer is the most powerful and immediate connection we have with the Almighty. We who are believers in Jesus Christ have a direct avenue to God. "Do not be anxious about anything, but in every situation, by prayer and petition, with thanksgiving, present your requests to God. And the peace of God, which transcends all understanding, will guard your hearts and your minds in Christ Jesus" (Philippians 4:6,7). "He will not let your foot slip — he who watches over you will not slumber; indeed, he who watches over Israel will neither slumber nor sleep"

(Psalms 121:3). The original, and the only true 24/7. And he means it.

It is good for the soul to spend time in prayer. Pray when there is no need to hurry. Take the time to relax, think, give thanks, express your love and wonder that the Lord God Almighty actually cares for you. Pray for those you love, individually for those you care for. Pray for those who have an eternal need for the Lord, but as yet have not accepted him as Lord. As you relax in prayer, many things and people, and events will come to your mind. Pray for those in harm's way, the military, the missionaries, Christians in hostile countries. Pray for the policemen in this country who so constantly are under attack, by the very people they are protecting. Pray that this country, which was once a strong Christian nation, will be able to return to the Lord. Pray that the evil and lies that are destroying our people will be overcome with truth, justice, and righteousness. Pray for yourself that the Lord, your God will bless, guide, provide, and heal you and direct your life. Pray that the Lord would grant you that most exquisite gift of being used by him. That your life might receive many eternal rewards because you are using the opportunities you have. God cares, and it is only he who gives to you what you have, and he will supply what you need. Many times in prayer we are unsure how to phrase it, or what words to use. If you were communicating with people, that would be a problem, but with God, he knows your mind and your heart, and he understands thoroughly your needs and desires. Paul tells us "In the same way, the Spirit helps us in our weakness. We do not know what we ought to pray for, but the Spirit himself intercedes for us through wordless groans. And he who searches our hearts knows the mind of the Spirit, because the Spirit intercedes for God's people in accordance with the will of God" (Romans 8:26, 27). As you call out to God, ask him to help us with our country. We are in constant need, because we are constantly under the attack of the evil one. With like mind, pray for Israel. Not only are we ask to pray for the peace of Jerusalem, but God has promised through Abraham, "I will bless those who bless you, and whoever curses you I will curse; and all peoples on earth will be blessed through you" (Genesis 12:3). Believe what he says, accept his intercession for you, and accept the blessing he has promised you for blessing Israel.

"Rejoice always, pray continually, give thanks in all circumstances; for this is God's will for you in Christ Jesus" (1 Thessalonians 5:16, 17). How can we pray continually? Don't we have other things to do? The way we pray continually, is the constant knowledge that the Holy Spirit of God indwells us all the time. We are never without his presence. It is somewhat like being with your loved one on a trip. This is, of course, our trip through life. As you travel, you will talk some, and there will be times of silence, but you are always together. Sometimes there will be thoughts of each other, without anything spoken, and at other times, a look, or a touch, but there is always the awareness of the constant presence. That kind of continual prayer with God is most peaceful. From time to time, and at any time a closeness with the Lord will be felt and the overwhelming thankfulness for who he is and what he has done gives peace. In addition to this blessing of his constant presence, we also pray for specifics. The care of our loved ones, concern for our nation and for other nations of the earth, and for the coming of the Lord Jesus Christ.

After returning to Jesus Christ after so many years of absence, and visiting many churches, one of the times I enjoyed the most was listening to the beautiful words and teachings of the old hymns. One hymn that struck my heart, because of my recent return, after being away for twenty-five years, was *Prayer is the Soul's Sincere Desire[1]*. I especially enjoyed the verses: "Pray'r is the burden of a sigh, The falling of a tear, The upward glancing of an eye, When none but God is near." And "Pray'r is the contrite sinner's voice, Returning from his ways; While angels in their songs rejoice And cry, 'Behold, he prays!'" It was like hearing the Lord say, "Welcome home!"

Some prayers are not given when you have an abundance of time to relax and meditate. Sometimes we need to send up an "arrow prayer". There isn't time to start with a preamble, there is only time to ask for help. Immediate help. Some examples are, when Peter saw the Lord walking on water in the Sea of Galilee, "Lord, if it's you," Peter replied, 'tell me to come to you on the water.' 'Come', he said. Then Peter got down out of the boat, walked on the water and came toward Jesus. 'but when he saw the wind, he was afraid and, beginning to sink, cried out, 'Lord, save me!'" (Matthew 14:28-30). It is acceptable, and prudent, whenever necessary, to offer a most sincere prayer to the Almighty, by screaming "LORD HELP!"

Another example of an arrow prayer is found when Nehemiah, a cup bearer for King Artaxerxes, who was deeply concerned about the state of Jerusalem, because it was in shambles, the temple was destroyed, and the city gates had been burned, and the walls had been broken through. Nehemiah had prayed in earnestness to God about receiving favor in the presence of the king. He desired help from the king, but to appear before the king with any expression other than happy, could engender the king's anger. When Nehemiah brought the King his wine, Nehemiah's face was sad. The king noticed his sad countenance and ask why? Nehemiah explained about the condition of Jerusalem. "The king said to me, 'What is it you want?' Then I prayed to the God of heaven, and I answered the king," (Nehemiah 2:4). The prayer must have been exceedingly short, but meaningful. It was not difficult for Nehemiah to know what to say quickly, since many prayers had been expressed to the Lord God many times over the previous days. He was ready to make his request to the Lord. His prayer was short, his prayer was heard, understood, and granted. To see the way King Artaxerxes magnanimously responded, please read the record in Nehemiah 2:1- 9

"Therefore confess your sins to each other and pray for each other so that you may be healed. The prayer of a righteous person is powerful and effective" (James 5:16). James is talking about righteous persons. Are you a righteous person? If you are a believer in Jesus Christ, then by the grace of God, you have the righteousness of Christ. That qualifies you.

There are many examples in the Bible where specific prayers are specifically answered. Some answered immediately, and some answered over time. Some that come to mind are: 1 Samuel 1:27 where Hanna prayed for a child to dedicate to the Lord, and she was given the child Samuel. Another is in 1 Kings 18:37 where Elijah prayed for and received fire from heaven to consume the sacrifice. And the amazing answer to Hezekiah's prayer in 2 Kings 20:1-6, when the Lord gives Hezekiah, who was dying, fifteen more years of life. Jesus tells us, "Ask and it will be given to you; seek and you will find; knock and the door will be opened to you. For everyone who asks receives; the one who seeks finds; and to the one who knocks, the door will be opened" (Matthew 7:7,8).

"Cast all your anxiety on him because he cares for you" (1Peter 5:7).

I am only one person, and do not have contact with that many others, but I know of many people, who consider themselves to be Christian, who seem to have no dedication to prayer. They seem to desire the separation of church and real life. That is, the other 167 hours of the week. Since I don't know their hearts, I pray that I'm wrong. Each of us needs to capitalize on this most powerful and available resource. Stay always in practice, you don't know when you will have an immediate need. (We always have immediate needs.)

Know that he desires our prayers, because our prayers to him are evidence of our faith. Know his promises to us:

"The righteous cry out, and the Lord hears them; he delivers them from all their troubles" (Psalm 34:17).

"So do not fear, for I am with you; do not be dismayed, for I am your God. I will strengthen you and help you; I will uphold you with my righteous right hand" (Isaiah 41:10).

"The Lord is my light and my salvation — whom shall I fear? The Lord is the stronghold of my life — of whom shall I be afraid?" (Psalm 27:1).

All through the Bible, prayers and petitions are offered to the Lord God. What an incredible resource, to think that we who are in Christ Jesus, can appeal directly to God. Because he hears our prayers, and knows our hearts and minds, may we be constantly aware of his nearness, and be in constant contact with him, the Almighty. He alone truly cares, and He alone is able. Pray continually by being constantly aware of God's presence in you.

Chapter 20

The Joy of Witnessing

Being a witness for Jesus Christ is the great commandment he gave to us when he left this earth to be with God in heaven. The most valuable possession of your life is your faith in Christ, and it cannot be lost or diminished by sharing it with others. In fact, the value is multiplied. Not all of us are called to be preachers, most of us would shy away from such responsibility. But in witnessing for Christ, you only have to be yourself. Your life is a constant and continuing witness to all those around you, showing them who you are and what you believe and value. If you are in Christ then people will know you as being honest, kind, and considerate. I pray that your life will be lived so that all the people who know you would know if they have a question about God, Jesus Christ, or eternal life, you would be a good and truthful source of information. They would have confidence that you are someone who would talk with them without being rude, insulting, condescending, or condemning, but open and honest, and with a serious concern for them. "But in your hearts revere Christ as Lord. Always be prepared to give an answer to everyone who asks you to give the reason for the hope that you have. But do this with gentleness and respect, keeping a clear conscience, so that those who speak maliciously against your good behavior in Christ may be ashamed of their slander" (1 Peter 3:15, 16).

Your lifestyle prepares your way to talk with people about your values. You might start with your family and closest friends. Possibly some or most of them are Christians, but if not, isn't it your desire for them to have the eternal gift of life that you have received? Do you know that those you love have this assurance of eternal life through their faith in Jesus Christ? Do you know it for sure? Have you talked with them about it. Have you tested their faith, and their doctrine of belief, or do you think, they are good people, you love them, and that is enough. Love them enough to ask them, and to make sure that they have true faith, and are not just deluded by some other gospel. Most all children and older students in high school or college are indoctrinated with worldly ideas that are godless. Know your foundation in the Bible. God's arguments are good, because they are true. Witnessing to others is no more than talking with them. In your conversation you will talk about the things you like. Mention your faith, or talk about your church, or quote the Bible regarding something in the general conversation. These small references might not be responded to by others, but they will probably make an impression on them.

When you read a good book, don't you want to tell others about it? When you see a good movie, don't you tell others? When you enjoy a good restaurant, don't you tell others so they can enjoy it also? Congratulations! You have been witnessing. You are sharing with others the joy you have received, and what is currently on your mind. You have merely talked about the things that you enjoy, and are important to you. If you spent more time reading and studying God's word in the Bible, if you spent more serious time thinking about and meditating on his word, and his promises, then that is what would be on your mind, and that is what you would be interested in sharing. It is better food than you experienced in the restaurant. It is truth, and it is life. We speak of what is on our mind. We love to speak about the things we know and understand. "A good man out of the good treasure of his heart brings forth good; and an evil man out of the evil treasure of his heart brings forth evil. For out of the abundance of the heart his mouth speaks" (Luke 6:45 NKJV). Those things that are important to us, we naturally desire to share with others.

Be yourself. Like the saying that I've heard attributed to Oscar Wilde: "Be yourself; everyone else is already taken". Trust what God has given you. You are unique. No one else in the whole world is you. It is your uniqueness that allows you to speak to some people who no one else can reach. Use your opportunities as they arise. A most important point is that you do not have to be a great orator or a great debater. Paul was one of the greatest evangelists ever, and just see what he says about his own ability. "When I came to you, I did not come with eloquence or human wisdom as I proclaimed to you the testimony about God. For I resolved to know nothing while I was with you except Jesus Christ and him crucified. I came to you in weakness with great fear, and trembling. My message and my preaching were not with wise and persuasive words, but with a demonstration of the Spirit's power, so that your faith might not rest on human wisdom, but on God's power" (1 Corinthians 2:1-5).

If Paul, the greatest evangelizing disciple, witnesses with fear and trembling, realizing his own weakness, and not having confidence in the ability to speak persuasively or with wisdom, but only knowing the story of Jesus Christ and him crucified, then we should not hesitate to witness just because we feel the same inadequacies. We like Paul must rely on the power and presence of God's Holy Spirit who indwells each believer. We are not alone. "The one who is in you is greater than the one who is in the world" (1 John 4:4). You can do this. "But you will receive power when the Holy Spirit comes on you; and you will be my witnesses in Jerusalem, and in all Judea and Samaria, and to the ends of the earth" (Acts 1:8).

Do not be guilty of saying, I can't, or I don't know how, that might be true, but it only means that you need to develop an attitude of eagerness to talk about God. For starters, just list two or three questions or comments you can make to start the conversation, then just talk about what you believe. Know the conclusion you are headed for. To explain that Jesus Christ is Lord, and eternal life is found only in him. This compares with playing baseball. Your goal is to score, but to do that you must get to first base.

188

Don't be discouraged. Even if you strike out, you will have made an impression. And besides that, you will have started a practice which will become easier and more normal in your daily conversation. There is a God, and he loves you, and wants the very best for you. Don't think this has to be done in one session. It might be, but it usually is not. You might only lay a part of the foundation. You might only add a brick or two where others have started. You might only give some encouragement. All you need to do is talk with people and offer a word or two about your faith, and most importantly, ask them about theirs. Listen. Respond in the way that only you can. The way God will lead you.

To be a good witness, you should first prepare. Know your Bible. As you read, underline, highlight, and write notes in the margin. When you find verses that are especially dear to you, memorize them. Yes you can. You can remember your name, your address and zip code, your phone number, etc. Those things were not automatically known, but had to be memorized. You memorized them because they were important. Items are memorized by rote. Memorized by going over them again and again. You don't need to memorize scripture exactly in order to use it and refer to it. Even if you forget the exact address in scripture, you will remember the concept. That's good.

Probably the most important part of preparation is prayer. Have a repeated request in your prayers that you might be a blessing to others by your willingness to share your faith. Pray that the way you live your life will be a witness. God answers prayers. This is one he will delight in.

Pray– before you have encounters – during – and after.
Meditate regularly on scripture.
Know what you have believed.
Have a genuine love for people, the love that Christ has for them.
Memorize scripture passages. Have at least two or three that you are confident in.
Be patient — gentle.
Do listen intently.
Encourage them to read the Bible.
When appropriate say "I don't know."

Witnessing is the greatest thing I know of, for receiving riches in heaven. Your attitude is judged by God, not just by outward appearances, but the attitude in your heart, because God looks on the heart. If you love righteousness and if you hate wickedness, you will be rewarded. "But let justice roll on like a river, righteousness like a never-failing stream!" (Amos 5:24). If you do that and love that, it will build up for you treasures in heaven. In the book of Ephesians, after telling us that we are saved by grace through faith in Christ, Paul tells us in verse 2:10 "For we are God's handiwork, created in Christ Jesus to do good works, which God prepared in advance for us to do." Think of that. The Lord has prepared in advance, good works for all believers who are saved by grace to do.

Going through life doing good works for others, is doing good works for God. It is clear that these works have nothing to do with our salvation, but they do lay up for us treasures in heaven. As you read the Bible, you will see the many ways we can honor him by doing good. Good works to family and friends, to neighbors, and to strangers. "For I was hungry and you gave me something to eat, I was thirsty and you gave me something to drink, I was a stranger and you invited me in, I needed clothes and you clothed me, I was sick and you looked after me, I was in prison and you came to visit me" (Matthew 25:35,36). For I was hungry . . . the unsaved people of this world have an enormous hunger in their lives for God. We have the opportunity to invite them to the table. If we imitate Jesus, and obey his commands, we honor him, and will be welcomed into his kingdom. I know of no greater work for God, than sharing our faith in Jesus with others.

Directions to Heaven

Chapter 21

Apostasy

IN THE NAME OF GOD, AMEN

These are the words that head the Mayflower Compact, signed in Cape Cod Bay on November 11, 1620. In the body of the document, it states their objective, To wit: "For the glory of God", and "for the advancement of the Christian faith".

On April 10, 1606, the first Virginia Charter proclaimed: "their Desires for the Furtherance of so noble a Work, which may, by the Providence of Almighty God, hereafter tend to the Glory of His Divine Majesty, in propagating of Christian Religion to such People, as yet live in Darkness and miserable Ignorance of the true Knowledge and Worship of God."

From the discovery of America by Christopher Columbus, to the founding of Jamestown in Virginia and the New Plymouth Colony at Cape Cod Bay, and all thirteen colonies, to the formal founding of our country in 1776, and for more than one hundred and fifty years after that, the United States has undoubtedly become the strongest Christian nation in the world. The US has also been the most successful exporter of Christianity to the world. Although the 1920s were known for their wild excesses, the 1930s brought us back closer to God as most of the nation prayed for their survival through the great depression, and the loss of farms and lives in the horrible dust storms. The second world war of the 1940s certainly brought us closer to God as once again we prayed for survival and victory over evil. The daily newspapers were rife with prayers to God, by everyone from citizens to President Franklin D. Roosevelt.

In the mid-1900s, prayer was eliminated from schools. The Bible has been disallowed in schools. Even the posting of the ten commandments has been outlawed by our court judges and justices. An onslaught of court cases has challenged every vestige of the Christian faith. Chaplains in the military were not allowed to pray in Jesus' name. The abortion of babies was made a legal practice. The institution of marriage was debased. It seems that nothing we have done as a nation has drawn us closer to God, but time and time again, change and change again, we drifted further away from God and his commands. This drifting away from our godly founding is a national apostasy. National apostasy is nothing more than the sum of individuals who have chosen to be apostate. It seems we are drawing close to a time when our freedom of religion will be modified if not removed from the constitution. The objections made in congress to this falling away from God, have been nothing more than the paper tigers of rhetoric.

The numbers of the opposition seem to be greater than the number of supporters. The people in congress who we have chosen to represent us have allowed this and caused this. Our court system, once the greatest and fairest in the world has, in many cases, become no more than political tyranny, by ignoring their oath to interpret the constitution, and in some cases, usurping the roll of congress by legislating laws into effect.

Apostasy, as a general term means the abandonment of a previous loyalty. In a religious sense means the renunciation of religious faith. For the Christian, it is the conscious, willful denial of their faith in Jesus Christ, the disbelief of his claims and teachings. Only the Lord knows when a person approaches or transgresses this boundary. For whatever we think apostasy is, I believe it to be a process, which if not dealt with by the individual, will culminate in spiritual death. However, I also find it inconceivable that any person alive cannot repent of sin, and ask forgiveness in Jesus' name.

The people who identify themselves as Christian in the United States has dropped from 77% down to 65% from the years 2009 to 2019. The people who claim to go to church monthly or more often has dropped from 54% to 45% over the same time period. In this same time frame, the religiously unaffiliated have shown an increase from 17% to 26%. These are huge numbers of people. These statistics are from the Pew Research Center.[1] The report from Pew Research stated that decline of Christianity in the

US continues at a rapid pace. It has been declining for many years. Many of the churches that have survived have done so by mitigating or ignoring good and faithful doctrine, or abandoning it. I have also read recently that church attendance in Great Britain had fallen to 7.5%. I believe that the evangelical presence in Europe is minuscule. So, how do you think our fulfillment of the Lord's great commission is going?

While large numbers of Christian churches in America desire to please people and make them comfortable, true doctrine is sometimes ignored. I cannot speak for all churches. There are many that I watch daily or weekly on television, that I believe are true to their calling. And besides that, I am not the one to judge because I know so little about all of this wonderful country, its many people, and many churches. I can only give my very limited opinion. But when entire church denominations refuse to identify sinful behavior as sinful, I do not feel the need to know each church to see that they are falling away. Woe to you pastors and teachers who encourage apostasy by not teaching righteousness.

It seems to me that the evidence I see is indicative of a nationwide (worldwide) rebellion or a falling away from God. That is the definition of the word apostasy. This current rebellion against God could be the prophesied rebellion in 2 Thessalonians chapter 2, that Paul declares must happen before the day of the Lord. This expression, the day of the Lord, refers to the last period of seven years

of the tribulation. It will be the final outpouring of God's wrath against all evil, and before the second coming of Jesus Christ spoken of in Zechariah 14.4. Paul explains to the church, that day has not happened yet. "Don't let anyone deceive you in any way, for that day will not come until the rebellion occurs and the man of lawlessness is revealed, the man doomed to destruction"
(2 Thessalonians 2:3).

So the order is: the rebellion (in some Bible translations it is called the *Apostasy*), which could be happening now, then the rapture of the church, then the revealing of the Antichrist and the rest of the seven years of tribulation, then the return of Christ Jesus in power and authority which will end Armageddon, then the millennium, followed by the second resurrection, then the great white throne judgment, and then the new heaven and the new earth.

The good news is that the "day of the Lord" is preceded by the rapture. Are you ready?

Directions to Heaven

Chapter 22

Consummation

The only true value in being alive is to receive eternal life in heaven.

Whatever your successes or failures, whatever your loves or disappointments, nothing in this world can last forever, except your soul, that can become eternal through faith in Jesus Christ.

If you have a saving faith in Jesus Christ as your Lord and savior, then your name is written in the Lamb's Book of Life. That Book of Life is a listing of everyone who believes in Jesus, and to whom will be given eternal life in a paradise, an eternal joy beyond description. Even Paul who was taken up to the third heaven, that he called it "paradise", only reported that: "He heard inexpressible things, things that man is not permitted to tell" (2 Corinthians 12:4).

The greatest meal you have ever enjoyed, only lasted for a short time, then you were hungry again. All people have a continual need to love and be loved. We each need to be recognized, and to be accepted. We need fulfillment in our lives. These important things, that we can only experience in a limited and a temporary way on earth, are provided for us perfectly and eternally in heaven by the God who made us.

Chapter 2, on salvation, explains how to get your name written in the Book of Life,

For Christian believers in Jesus Christ, it is of the highest importance that you live your life honoring God. We will not all enter into heaven on equal basis. Those who have lived a life of obeying the Lord, and doing his will, can enter heaven and hear the words "Well done, good and faithful servant" (Matthew 25:21), and receive your eternal rewards. But however you enter, be there! Please do not ignore this most precious eternal gift to you personally, from Jesus Christ himself.

"For the wages of sin is death, but the gift of God is eternal life in Christ Jesus our Lord" (Romans 6:23).

Fortunately, for each of us, Jesus said: "I have not come to call the righteous, but sinners to repentance" (Luke 5:31).

Godspeed.

References

==

Chapter 1 – Beginnings
1. William J. Federer, For God and Country (Green Tree Press, 1960) p.70
2.https://en.wikipedia.org/wiki/Gone_with_the_wind_%28film%29   January 30, 2018
3. Alexis De Tocqueville, Democracy in America (Adlard and Saunders; George Dearborn & Co., 1838) p. 76

Chapter 2 – Salvation
1. Tulsa Beacon, (Biggs Communications, Inc. Tulsa, Oklahoma, 74153) April 18, 2018, Letters to The Editor

Chapter 4 – To Judge or not to Judge
1. The Wycliffe Bible Commentary, (Moody Press, 1990), p. 1187

Chapter 5 – Nicer than God
1. https://news.yahoo.com/pope-shifts-church-death-penalty-103647335.htmlMarch 5, 2019
2. Dave Hunt, *A Woman Rides The Beast* (Harvest House Publishers, 1994)
3. Malachi Martin, *The Decline and Fall of the Roman Church*, (G. P. Putnam's Sons, 1981)

Chapter 6 – The Rapture
1. The Bible Knowledge Commentary (Victor Books, 1987), pp. 706-707

Chapter 9 – Time
1. Omar Khayyam, *The Rubaiyat Of Omar Khayyam (Publisher and publishing date – unknown)* Edward Fitzgerald – First Version – Chapter LIII

Chapter 12 – Prayer
1. Wilhelm A. F. Schulthes, Church Service Hymns (The Rodeheaver, Hall-Mack Company, 1962) hymn number 267

Chapter 20 – Apostasy
1. Pew Research Center https://www.pewforum.org/2019/10/17/in-u-s-decline-of-christianity-continues-at-rapid-pace/ February 22, 2021

www.ingramcontent.com/pod-product-compliance
Lightning Source LLC
Chambersburg PA
CBHW021628120626
46545CB00002B/444